1780

1850

1900

NORTH CAROLINA
TAPROOTS

Other books by Paul Shields Crane

Korean Patterns (1967, Fifth Edition 1998)

Tennessee's Troubled Roots: County Jails of Tennessee (1979, coauthored with Sophie Mongtomery Crane)

Tennessee Taproots: Courthouses of Tennessee (1976, revised edition 1996, coauthored with Sophie Montgomery Crane)

North Carolina
TAPROOTS

Courthouses of
North Carolina
Paul Shields Crane

HILLSBORO PRESS
Franklin, Tennessee

First Edition

Printed in the United States of America

02   01   00   99   98   1   2   3   4   5

Library of Congress Catalog Card Number: 97-75414

ISBN: 1–57736–042–7

Cover by Gary Bozeman

Cover photos (top to bottom): Union Courthouse (old), Chowan Courthouse, and Edgecombe Courthouse.

Endsheets are from North Carolina 1830 Index (Accelerated Index System, Inc., Bountiful, Utah).

Published by
HILLSBORO PRESS
an imprint of
PROVIDENCE HOUSE PUBLISHERS
238 Seaboard Lane • Franklin, Tennessee 37067
800-321-5692

TO my wife
Sophie Montgomery Crane

North Carolina County Seats

County Seat	County	County Seat	County
Albemarle	Stanly	Louisburg	Franklin
Asheboro	Randolph	Lumberton	Robeson
Asheville	Buncombe	Manteo	Dare
Bakersville	Mitchell	Marion	McDowell
Bayboro	Pamlico	Marshall	Madison
Beaufort	Carteret	Mocksville	Davie
Bolivia	Brunswick	Monroe	Union
Boone	Watauga	Morganton	Burke
Brevard	Transylvania	Murphy	Cherokee
Bryson City	Swain	Nashville	Nash
Burgaw	Pender	New Bern	Craven
Burnsville	Yancey	Newland	Avery
Camden	Camden	Newton	Catawba
Carthage	Moore	Oxford	Granville
Charlotte	Mecklenburg	Pittsboro	Chatham
Clinton	Sampson	Plymouth	Washington
Columbia	Tyrrell	Raeford	Hoke
Columbus	Polk	Raleigh	Wake
Concord	Cabarrus	Robbinsville	Graham
Currituck	Currituck	Rockingham	Richmond
Danbury	Stokes	Roxboro	Person
Dobson	Surry	Rutherfordton	Rutherford
Durham	Durham	Salisbury	Rowan
Edenton	Chowan	Sanford	Lee
Elizabeth City	Pasquotank	Shelby	Cleveland
Elizabethtown	Bladen	Smithfield	Johnston
Fayetteville	Cumberland	Snow Hill	Greene
Franklin	Macon	Sparta	Alleghany
Gastonia	Gaston	Statesville	Iredell
Gatesville	Gates	Swan Quarter	Hyde
Goldsboro	Wayne	Sylva	Jackson
Graham	Alamance	Tarboro	Edgecombe
Greensboro	Guilford	Taylorsville	Alexander
Greenville	Pitt	Trenton	Jones
Halifax	Halifax	Troy	Montgomery
Hayesville	Clay	Wadesboro	Anson
Henderson	Vance	Warrenton	Warren
Hendersonville	Henderson	Washington	Beaufort
Hertford	Perquimans	Waynesville	Haywood
Hillsborough	Orange	Wentworth	Rockingham
Jackson	Northampton	Whiteville	Columbus
Jacksonville	Onslow	Wilkesboro	Wilkes
Jefferson	Ashe	Williamston	Martin
Kenansville	Duplin	Wilmington	New Hanover
Kinston	Lenoir	Wilson	Wilson
Laurinburg	Scotland	Windsor	Bertie
Lenoir	Caldwell	Winston-Salem	Forsyth
Lexington	Davidson	Winton	Hertford
Lillington	Harnett	Yadkinville	Yadkin
Lincolnton	Lincoln	Yanceyville	Caswell

Introduction

Almost every citizen in a county knows where the courthouse is. The courthouse is where your marriage license is issued, where you go to check on the deed to your home, complain about the potholes in the streets, and at some time, God forbid, possibly be hauled into court to face a judge. This handy guidebook will not keep you out of jail, but it may help introduce you to the counties of North Carolina: when they were formed, how they got their names, places of interest, sights worth visiting, and fun places to check out. For the newcomer to the state, the information may be helpful in considering the best place to locate a residence, start a new business, sell bubble gum, or even retire. This book is a peg on which to hang one's memory and add to the pleasure of being in North Carolina.

One of my first projects when I move to a new state is to take a tour and visit all the counties. Then I use the courthouse as a symbol by which to remember each county. The courthouse often reflects the economic, educational, cultural, and artistic level of the county, or the amount of "pork" the legislators were able to attract to build a grand temple of justice. Courthouses teach us history: seventy-four of the one hundred are on the *National Register of Historic Places*. Since the state was founded in 1776, forty-one courthouses have burned—insurance agents might take note.

A bit of history may set the stage. Christopher Columbus received a Papal Bull in 1492 claiming all the western hemisphere for Spain. He set sail heading west, following the latitude line to China. Navigational technology in Columbus's time was incapable of determining longitude. When he sighted land, Columbus assumed it to be India, and he called the natives "Indians" since they did not resemble his concept of the Chinese. He had discovered a vast land blocking his route to the "Center of the Universe" China.

John Cabot (Giovanni Ca-bo-to, *ca*1450–1499), an Italian navigator in the service of the English under Henry VII, claimed to have touched the Carolinas in 1497–1498; however, some dispute this claim. Amerigo Vespucci (1454–1512), an Italian navigator and explorer, got the credit, and the new world was named *America* in his honor. In 1524 Giovanni da Verrazano (*ca*1485–1528), an Italian in the service of France, discovered Cape Fear on the North Carolina coast; New York's famous Verrazano Bridge was named in his memory. Not until 1585 did Sir Walter Raleigh (1554–1618), an English navigator and historian, attempt to settle the first colony in North Carolina in what is now Dare County on Roanoke Island. This became known as the "lost colony" when it disappeared without a trace. Some speculate that the colonists, tired of waiting for Raleigh to return from a trip to England, took to the sea to return home and vanished.

Eventually Indians were pushed back by settlers, and the area of North Carolina became part of the British colonies until the American Revolution of 1776 won independence from England. During the Civil War of 1861–1865, North Carolina was a part of the Confederate States of America, but was brought back into the Union at the end of the war. One of the by-products of the Civil War was the rapid development of the tobacco industry, a major element in the agricultural activity of the state. Some astute Southern observers had noted that the Federal soldiers rushed to secure the fine tobacco leaves they enjoyed smoking and chewing. Thus, a major industry (and a troublesome health problem) was born when in 1875, Richard Joshua Reynolds, a young Virginian, rode into Winston on a horse to find a place to build the first major cigarette factory in North Carolina. A monument across from the Forsyth County Courthouse honors the memory of the founder of the R. J. Reynolds Tobacco Company, a basis for much of the wealth in the area.

In 1995 I decided to repeat in North Carolina what my wife and I had done in a previous book, *Tennessee Taproots: Courthouses of Tennessee*, Hillsboro Press, 1996. I set out to visit each of the one hundred counties in North Carolina to learn what I could about the scenery, geography, flowers, history, economics, educational levels, cultural advantages, health facilities, crime and punishment, number of live births and deaths in a recent year, and major products of each county. The basic information in this guidebook keeps me from being a complete dummy when North Carolinians talk about places and things happening in the state. I can at least say "I have been there and have a picture of each courthouse to prove it." I am becoming acclimated to the delightful environment and am proud to be a registered voter and taxpayer of the state of North Carolina.

No two counties are alike. The smallest in size is Chowan, a mere 180 square miles. Sampson County is the largest, with 963 square miles The state slopes upward from the coastal counties through the Piedmont to the western Appalachian mountains. Elevations range from Hyde County at 10 feet above sea level to Avery County at 3,589 feet. Density of population varies from a high in Mecklenburg of 1,082.2 persons per square mile to Hyde County with 8.7 persons per square mile.

According to the North Carolina State Data Center, in 1995 there were 7,197,044 residents of North Carolina. In 1995, of 3,476,600 registered voters in the state, 2,197,133 were Democrats, and 1,291,753 were registered Republicans. In ninety of the one hundred counties, the Democrats were in the majority; in only a few of the counties were voters almost politically balanced. In 1995, 3,478,600 citizens were employed and 157,600 were unemployed; an unemployment rate for the state of 4.1 percent. The unemployment rate ranged from 1.9 percent in Orange County with Wake and Randolph close behind at 2.4 percent, to Graham County with 17.3 percent and Swain County with 19.8 percent. The average income per person in 1995 for the state was $20,913 per person. The highest average income was $28,010 per year in Mecklenburg County; the lowest was in Hoke County, $12,583. A number of the counties had a nearly equal racial mix of whites and African Americans. Significant American Indian communities were reported in some western counties. Rising Asian and Latino populations were also noted.

The North Carolina climate is mostly benign, the scenery is spectacular, the natives are gracious, and the living is easy. This brief introduction will alert the traveler to some of the historic and scenic splendors that might otherwise be missed while speeding through North Carolina on a super highway. I hope that for students, this book may open new vistas to the opportunities in North Carolina.

I am deeply indebted to Eaelean Strickland, Office of State Planning, Raleigh, North Carolina, and to Claudia R. Brown, Supervisor, Survey and Planning Branch, State Historic Preservation Office. I give special thanks to Andy Miller, Mary Bray Wheeler, Jennifer Thomas, Debbie Sims, and Trinda Cole of Hillsboro Press for their editing and book design skills. Above all, my wife, Sophie Montgomery Crane, who put this manuscript in shape, corrected my many errors, edited the manuscript, and was my computer expert. I am also indebted to my son-in-law, Dr. Randy Adams, for his patient computer expertise.

 **Alamance County** was established in 1849 from Orange County. *Alamance* is an Indian word for the county's "blue clay," which has a distinctive odor known locally as the "Piedmont scent." Graham was named for General Joe Graham of Revolutionary fame.

The first courthouse was built in 1849 and remodeled in 1882, 1888, and 1889. Replaced in 1924 at a cost of $250,000, the old courthouse received a $1.2 million face-lift in 1996 and is on the *National Register of Historic Places*. A criminal courts building was built in 1974.

Alamance County is drained by the Haw River. In 1771 at the Alamance Battle Ground, the "Regulators," a group of 2,000 homesteaders, met the 1,000-strong British, in a battle that ended the "War of Regulation" and struck the first blow for American liberty, five years before the Declaration of Independence.

> **Census:** 1950—71,220; 1995—115,548
> **Per capita income:** $18,647
> **Land area:** 434 square miles; elev. 656 ft.
> **Of Interest:** Elon College and Alamance Community College in Graham. Alamance Historical Museum in Burlington. *The Sword of Peace*, annual dramatic performance, Snow Camp.

 **Alexander County** was established in 1847 from Iredell, Caldwell, and Wilkes Counties and named in honor of William J. Alexander of Mecklenburg County, who had been speaker of England's House of Commons. Taylorsville was named for President Zachary Taylor.

The first courthouse was built in 1848; the second, built in 1902, burned in 1967. The present courthouse was built in 1970; B. F. Smith Fireproof Construction Co. was the builder.

Alexander County is drained by the Catawba River, and Lake Hickory forms the southern border. Various gemstones are found in the county.

Census: 1950—14,544; 1995—30,180
Per capita income: $16,771
Land area: 259 square miles; elev. 1,247 ft.
Of Interest: Natural Heritage Site and Cultural Treasure—Emerald Hollow Gem Mine, which features hiddenite and other semiprecious stones. Industry—Furniture, food, and textiles support half the work force. Produce—tobacco and broilers.

![Alexander County Courthouse]

Alexander County Seat—Taylorsville, North Carolina 28681   5

Alleghany County was established in 1859 from Ashe County. *Alleghany,* an Indian name for the Alleghany River, is said to mean "a fine river." Sparta is named for the ancient Greek city.

The first court met in the Methodist Church because the Civil War delayed the construction of the courthouse until 1867. In 1878 a new courthouse was built. A third courthouse, built in 1910, burned in 1932. In 1933 the present courthouse was designed by Harry Barton; construction was by the Fowler-Jones Lumber Company at a cost of $17,000. This courthouse is on the *National Register of Historic Places.*

Alleghany County has over 20,000 acres of state and national parks. Among these are Grayson Highlands State Park, Doughton Park, Cumberland State Park, New River State Park, and the Blue Ridge Parkway.

Census: 1950—8,155; 1995—9,581
Per capita income: $15,416
Land area: 230 square miles; elev. 2,939 ft.
Of Interest: The New River dips into the northern area of the county, and the New River State Park is a Natural Heritage Site. Stone Mountain State Park is easily identified by a 600-foot stone dome.

Anson County was established in 1748 from Bladen County and named for Lord George Anson, the British admiral who,

for a number of years, protected commerce along the coast from pirates. Admiral Anson was also famous for having circumnavigated the globe. Wadesboro was named in honor of Thomas Wade, a Revolutionary officer from Salisbury.

The first courthouse, built in 1755 in Mount Pleasant, was torn down in 1785 and moved to Wadesboro, where it became a private residence. A log courthouse, built in 1785 in Wadesboro, was replaced in 1830 by a brick courthouse. This courthouse burned in 1868, and was promptly rebuilt. In 1912 a new building was designed by Wheeler and Stern, the same architects who designed the courthouses of Stokes, Duplin, and Randolph Counties.

Anson County is drained by the Pee Dee River; the river was given the Catawba Indian name *pi'ri*, meaning "something good." Blewett Falls Lake has provided hydroelectric power since 1907.

Census: 1950—26,781; 1995—23,848
Per capita income: $15,265
Land area: 533 square miles; elev. 423 ft.
Of Interest: Schools—Anson Community College in Polkton. Produce—soybeans, cotton, peaches, and beef cattle.

Anson County Seat—Wadesboro, North Carolina 28170

 **Ashe County** was established in 1799 and named for Governor Samuel Ashe, Revolutionary patriot, three-term governor, and a North Carolina judge. Jefferson was named for President Thomas Jefferson.

The first courthouse, constructed in 1800, was replaced by a brick courthouse in 1833. The present fireproof courthouse was built in 1904 at a cost of $20,000. The architects, Wheeler and Runge of Charlotte, built similar courthouses in Alleghany, Avery, Iredell, Randolph, Scotland, and Stokes Counties. The Ashe County Courthouse is on the *National Register of Historic Places*.

The Blue Ridge Parkway follows the boundary of Ashe County with Wilkes County. Both the north and south forks of the New River wander through the county. A section of this river, as it flows through Mt. Jefferson State Park, is designated both a federal and a state "Wildlife Scenic River." Mt. Jefferson looms over the county seat.

Ashe County has two gems of art. At St. Mary's Episcopal Church near West Jefferson, built in 1905, are religious frescoes by the noted artist Ben Long, showing "Mary Great with Child" and stained glass windows and frescoes of the life of Christ. A few miles away just off the Skyland Parkway at Glendale Springs is the Holy Trinity Church with a dramatic fresco of the "Last Supper" and a basement level Columbarium filled with beautiful vases holding the ashes of departed members, arranged in a rock garden, which can be viewed through a glass door. Religious art at its best.

Census: 1950—21,878; 1995—22,998
Per capita income: $15,778
Land area: 427 square miles; elev. 2,900 ft.
Of Interest: Natural Heritage Sites—Bluff Mountain, the New River State Park, and Mt. Jefferson State Park. Cultural Treasure—The Blue Ridge Mountain Frescoes.

Avery County was established in 1911 and named for Colonel Waightstill Avery, Revolutionary soldier and attorney general of North Carolina, who owned the land now occupied by the town of Newland.

The courthouse was completed in 1913 at a cost of $25,800; architects were Wheeler and Runge of Charlotte. The Avery County Courthouse is on the *National Register of Historic Places*.

Avery County is drained by the Linville and South Toe Rivers. Pisgah National Forest occupies half of the county. The Appalachian Trail passes along the west side of the county. Rock formations, perhaps over one billion years old, are said to be the oldest in the world. The virgin Fraser Fir Forest at Banner Elk is awesome. Sugar Mountain and Beech Mountain ski resorts are popular in the winter. During the last week of May, the Rhododendron Gardens near the summit of Roan Mountain are one of the great splendors of nature.

Census: 1950—13,352; 1995—15,160
Per capita income: $16,813
Land area: 247 square miles; elev. 3,589 ft.
Of Interest: Schools—Lees-McRae College in Banner Elk. Natural Heritage Sites—Grandfather and Roan Mountains. Cultural Treasure—Linville Historic District.

Avery County Seat—Newland, North Carolina 28657

Beaufort County was established in 1705 from Bath County. Originally known as Pamptecough, it was named for Henry Somerset, Duke of Beaufort, who became one of the Lords Proprietors in 1709. Washington became the county seat in 1785 and has the distinction of being the first place in the United States to be named in honor of President George Washington.

The county seat was first located in Bath, the oldest town in North Carolina (incorporated in 1704). A courthouse was built of wood in 1706 and replaced in 1756. Another courthouse, built in 1786 in Washington, served until the present courthouse was built in 1971. The old courthouse is on the *National Register of Historic Places* and now serves as a library and meeting hall.

The Tar River flows into the Pamlico River, dividing the county and forming what resembles the open jaws of an alligator. A free ferry crosses the Pamlico River near Bayview on Highway 306. Goose Creek State Park is known for its sandy beaches along the Pamlico River. The Intracoastal Waterway passes through Goose Creek, the Pungo River, and across the Pamlico River. Edward Teach, known as "Blackbeard the Pirate," met his violent end in Bath in 1718.

Census: 1950—37,174; 1995—43,442
Per capita income: $15,166
Land area: 831 square miles; elev. 11 ft.
Of Interest: Schools—Beaufort County Community College in Washington. National Historic Landmark—The Palmer-Marsh House in Bath.

Bertie County was established in 1722 and named for brothers James and Henry Bertie, who became Lords Proprietors in 1728. Windsor was established in 1774 and named for Windsor Castle near London.

Previous county seats were at St. John's in 1724 (now in Hertford County) and Wolfenden (two miles north of Windsor), where a second courthouse was built in 1743. The present courthouse was built in Windsor in 1887; wings were added in 1941. The Bertie County Courthouse is listed on the *National Register of Historic Places*.

Bertie County is bordered on the west and south by the Roanoke River and on the east by the Chowan River and Albemarle Sound. The Cashie River flows by Windsor. The county is heavily forested. The Hope Plantation is on land granted to the Hobson family in the 1720s by the Lords Proprietors of the Carolina Colony.

Census: 1950—26,439; 1995—20,648
Per capita income: $14,169
Land area: 693 square miles; elev. 10 ft.
Of Interest: Industry—apparel manufacturing.

Bladen County was established in
1734 and named for Martin Bladen, a member of the Board of Trade and a commissioner in charge of colonial affairs. Elizabethtown was established in 1773 on the Cape Fear River.

The first courthouse, built in 1783, burned in 1802. The second courthouse, 1802, burned in 1893, was rebuilt, and burned in 1925. Rebuilt and enlarged, this courthouse was demolished in 1963. Federal funds and the sale of bonds financed the present courthouse.

The county has many areas suitable for water sports and fishing: White Lake, Jones Lake State Park, Singletary Lake State Park, Fear River, Colly Creek, South River, and many smaller lakes.

Census: 1950—29,703; 1995—29,807
Per capita income: $14,507
Land area: 879 square miles; elev. 121 ft.
Of Interest: Schools—Bladen Community College in Dublin. Produce—peanuts and hogs.

 **Brunswick County** was established in 1764 and named for King George I, Duke of Brunswick. Bolivia, formed in 1912, became the county seat in 1978. The Postmaster is said to have named the town from the word "Bolivia," seen on a sack of fertilizer shipped in from the South American country.

The first courthouse was built of wood at Lockwood's Folly in 1764. The county seat was moved to Smithville in 1808, where a wooden courthouse was erected. By 1840 the county had outgrown the old courthouse, and a new edifice was built in 1844. In 1889 the name Smithville was changed to Southport. Following a fire in 1922, extensive renovations were made. The courthouse in Southport is on the *National Register of Historic Places*. In 1978 a large one-story county government complex was built in a rural setting on the southwest edge of Bolivia.

Brunswick County is bordered on the east by the Outer Banks and the Atlantic Ocean, on the north by the Cape Fear River, and on the west to the South Carolina line by the Waccamaw River. Cape Fear Sound separates the Outer Banks from the mainland. Access to the ocean is provided by inlets: Tubbs, Shallotte, Lockwood's Folly, and Corncake. Popular beaches on the Outer Banks include Holden Beach, Long Beach, Ocean Isle, and Sunset Beach. Fort Fisher was the last major stronghold of the Confederacy. A nuclear power plant at Southport is a key to future growth.

> **Census:** 1950—19,238; 1995—60,746
> **Per capita income:** $14,834
> **Land area:** 873 square miles; elev. 40 ft.
> **Of Interest:** Schools—Brunswick Community College in Supply. Tourist Attractions—U.S.S. *North Carolina* Battleship Memorial, Brunswick Town State Historical Site, Orton Plantation Gardens, and the Old Brunswick ruins. Produce—tobacco, corn, soybeans, and the largest production of oysters in the state.

 ***Buncombe County*** was established in 1791 from Burke and Rutherford Counties and named for Colonel Edward Buncombe, a Revolutionary soldier who died in 1778 in Philadelphia while a paroled prisoner of war. Asheville was named for Governor Samuel Ashe (1796–1798).

Buncombe County has had seven courthouses. The first was built in 1792 in Morristown, which was renamed Asheville in 1797. The second courthouse was built in the early 1800s and the third 1825–1833. The fourth, built in 1850, was destroyed by fire in 1865 and replaced by the fifth, a small temporary building. The sixth courthouse was built in 1903. From 1923–1928 the seventh courthouse, a seventeen-story building, was erected at a cost of $1,000,000. Frank P. Milburn was the architect. The Buncombe County Courthouse is on the *National Register of Historic Places*.

Buncombe County has been a major resort area for over one hundred years. The Pisgah National Forest and the Blue Ridge Parkway are natural attractions. Summer camps for boys and girls, conference centers, and retirement facilities bring many to the region. Religious conference centers include Blue Ridge (YMCA), Christmount (Disciples), the Cove (Billy Graham), In the Oaks (Episcopalian), Montreat (Presbyterian), and Ridgecrest (Baptist).

Census: 1950—124,403; 1995—188,912
Per capita income: $19,355
Land area: 646 square miles; elev. 2,216 ft.
Of Interest: Schools—Montreat College in Montreat, UNC-Asheville, and Warren Wilson College in Swannanoa. Attractions—The Grove Park Inn Resort and the Park Place (Education, Arts, Science) Center. National Historic Landmarks and Cultural Treasures—George Vanderbilt's Biltmore Estates, with gardens and winery; and the home of author Thomas Wolfe, whose most famous work was *Look Homeward Angel*. Natural Heritage Sites—the Folk Art Center, Young Men's Institute, St. Lawrence Catholic Church, Zebulon Vance's birthplace, Carolina Arboretum, Nature Center, and Craggy Gardens.

 **Burke County** was established in 1777 from Rowan County and named for Dr. Thomas Burke, a member of the Continental Congress and governor of North Carolina (1781–1782). Morganton was named for General Daniel Morgan of the Revolutionary Army.

The first courthouse, built of logs in 1785, was replaced in 1791. In 1820 a building was erected for the clerks of the court, which, along with the 1791 courthouse, served until replaced in 1833 by a two-story courthouse with a cupola. Court records were burned during the last year of the Civil War by Federal raiders under General George Stoneman. In 1976 a modern courthouse, designed by J. T. Peagram, was erected one block east of the old courthouse. The old courthouse is on the *National Register of Historic Places*.

The Pisgah National Forest and the Blue Ridge Parkway occupy part of the county. The Catawba River, Lake Rhodhiss, and Lake James are popular recreational areas. The drama *From This Day Forward* is enacted at the Valdese Foundation during the summer months.

Census: 1950—45,518; 1995—81,372
Per capita income: $16,633
Land area: 506 square miles; elev. 1,182 ft.
Of Interest: Schools—Western Piedmont Community College in Morganton. Natural Historic Sites—South Mountain State Park and Linville Gorge and Falls. Cultural Treasures—The Waldesian Museum, the Waldesian Presbyterian Church, and the Valdese Foundation.

Cabarrus County was established in 1792 and named for Stephen Cabarrus, four-time speaker of the British House of Commons. Concord was named for Concord, Massachusetts.

In January 1793, court met in Robert Russell's home. A wooden courthouse was built in 1795 and served until 1826 when a larger brick courthouse was constructed. This courthouse was enlarged in 1872 and destroyed by fire in 1875. Rebuilt, it served until 1974 and is on the *National Register of Historic Places*. A sleek modern courthouse, designed by George A. Griffin of Concord, was built in 1974.

The Rocky River flows through the county.

Census: 1950—63,783; 1995—110,407
Per capita income: $18,799
Land area: 360 square miles; elev. 704 ft.
Of Interest: Schools—Barber-Scotia College, a Presbyterian college in Concord. National Historic Landmark and North Carolina Historical Site—Reed Gold Mine near Stanfield. Produce—dairy products and cattle. Industry—Kannapolis is the home of Cannon towels.

Cabarrus County Seat—Concord, North Carolina 28025

Caldwell County was established in 1841 and named for Joseph Caldwell, first president of the University of North Carolina. Lenoir was named for William Lenoir, a Revolutionary War hero of the Battle of Kings Mountain.

The first courthouse was built in 1848 and remodeled in 1910. In 1929 Hartley and Smith renovated and enlarged the courthouse at a cost of $170,000. In 1990 a new courthouse was built and attached to the 1929 building. The architects were Northwest Associates, and Hanwood Beche Company, the contractor. Caldwell County Courthouse is on the *National Register of Historic Places.*

Pisgah National Forest and Lake Rhodhiss are partly in Caldwell County.

Census: 1950—43,353; 1995—73,706
Per capita income: $16,674
Land area: 476 square miles; elev. 1,182 ft.
Of Interest: Schools—Caldwell Community College and Technical Institute in Hudson. Cultural Treasure—Fort Defiance. Tourist Attractions—County Heritage Museum, Tuttle State Park, Tweetsie Railroad, and Powderhorn Mountain Resort. Industry—textiles and furniture. Broyhill and Bernhardt's furniture companies together make Caldwell County the "Furniture Capital of the South." Produce—chickens, corn, and tobacco.

Caldwell County Seat—Lenoir, North Carolina 28645   23

 **Camden County** was established in 1777 and named for Charles Pratt, Earl of Camden, a strong supporter of the American colonies in the British Parliament. The county seat is also named Camden.

The courthouse site was purchased in 1782. The first courthouse burned about 1846. Rebuilt in 1847, the courthouse is still in use today and is on the *National Register of Historic Places*.

This tidewater county is almost surrounded by waters of the Pasquotank River, the Swamp Canal, and the North River. The Great Dismal Swamp occupies much of the county. The county is entirely rural.

Census: 1950—5,223; 1995—6,320
Per capita income: $14,521
Land area: 239 square miles; elev. 10 ft.
Of Interest: Produce—corn, soybeans, wheat, and hogs. Industry—some manufacturing.

Carteret County was established in
1722 and named for Sir John Carteret, Earl of Granville, one of the colonial Lords Proprietors. Beaufort was established in 1723 and named for Henry, Duke of Beaufort.

The first courthouse was built in Beaufort in 1722. A second courthouse was built in 1767 and a third in 1832. The present courthouse was built in 1907; in recent years an additional wing was added. Herbert W. Simpson was the architect. The Carteret County Courthouse is on the *National Register of Historic Places*. Beaufort is a historic seaport as well as the center of county government and has many beautiful homes along the waterfront. Beaufort is pronounced Bofort in North Carolina; in South Carolina, Beaufort is pronounced Bufort.

The county faces the Atlantic Ocean. The mainland is separated from the Outer Banks by Bogue Sound, Back Sound, and Core Sound. The Neuse River and Pamlico Sound form the northern border. The Intracoastal Waterway runs through Bogue Sound, turns north through Newport River, and cuts through the county to Adams Creek on the Neuse River. Large areas of the county are taken up with the Croatan Game Land, Pocosin Wilderness, and the Cedar Island National Game Refuge. A bridge over the Newport River connects Beaufort with Morehead City, a major port.

Census: 1950—23,059; 1995—57,716
Per capita income: $16,175
Land area: 532 square miles; elev. 9 ft.
Of Interest: Schools—Carteret Community College in Morehead City. Tourist Attractions—Cape Lookout National Seashore, Theodore Roosevelt State Park, Fort Macon State Park, the Marine Museum, and the Marine Resource Center. Produce—soybeans, tobacco, phosphate, and lumber.

Carteret County Seat—Beaufort, North Carolina 28516 25

Caswell County was established in 1777 and named for Richard Caswell, a member of the Continental Congress, major general in the Revolutionary War, and Carolina's first governor following independence. Yanceyville was named for Bartlett Yancey, a prominent public figure in the area.

The first courthouse was constructed in Leasburg around 1788. The second wooden courthouse was built in Yanceyville and replaced in 1831–1833 by a brick courthouse, which burned. A brick courthouse was built (1858–1861) and is on the *National Register of Historic Places*. A new courthouse, designed by Echols-Sparger and Associates, was built in 1975. In 1870 the county was placed under martial law by the governor when State Senator John W. ("Chicken") Stephens was murdered in the courthouse by the Ku Klux Klan, who accused him of being a carpetbagger.

Caswell County is in rolling country in the northern Piedmont. The Dan River dips into the county. Part of Hyco Lake occupies the eastern part of the county.

Census: 1950—20,870; 1995—21,254
Per capita income: $14,480
Land area: 435 square miles; elev. 619 ft.
Of Interest: National Historic Landmark—Union Tavern (Thomas Day House) in Milton. Produce—tobacco, wheat, corn, and soybeans. Industry—textiles, apparel, and chemicals.

Caswell County Seat—Yanceyville, North Carolina 37379   27

Catawba County was established in 1842 and named for the Catawba Indian tribe living in the area. Newton was named for Sir Isaac Newton, the British mathematician and physicist.

The first brick courthouse was built in 1844. Wings were added in 1904 and a vault built in 1923. A second courthouse, erected in 1924, is on the *National Register of Historic Places*. A large new courthouse and justice center was built in 1980 in a new location on the edge of the city.

The Catawba River and Lake Norman form the northern and eastern boundaries of the county.

Census: 1950—61,086; 1995—126,154
Per capita income: $20,469
Land area: 406 square miles; elev. 996 ft.
Of Interest: Schools—Catawba Valley Community College in Hickory. Cultural Treasures—Catawba County Museum, the Bunker Hill Covered Bridge, and Murray's Mill. Produce—corn, wheat, soybeans, dairy, beef cattle, and poultry. Industry—The Hickory Furniture Market is a major outlet for the large furniture industry in Hickory.

Catawba County Seat—Newton, North Carolina 28658

Chatham County was established
in 1770 from Orange County and named for William Pitt, Earl of Chatham, a defender of American causes in the British Parliament during the Revolution. Pittsboro was also named to honor William Pitt.

A frame courthouse was built in 1771 on Miles Scurlock's farm and abandoned in 1787 when Pittsboro became the county seat. A wooden courthouse was built in Pittsboro and replaced in 1843 with a brick building. In 1881 a new courthouse was erected at a cost of $10,666, renovated in 1930 by adding a story, and extensively remodeled in 1959 at a cost of $130,000. This courthouse is on the *National Register of Historic Places*. In 1985 a large new courthouse was built across the street from the old courthouse.

Chatham County is largely rural. The Haw and Rocky Rivers, the New Hope Reservoir, and the B. Everett Jordan Lake are located in the county.

Census: 1950—25,392; 1995—42,870
Per capita income: $19,787
Land area: 707 square miles; elev. 409 ft.
Of Interest: Produce—tobacco, corn, and soybeans. Industry—Clay, stone, and glass products are manufactured.

 **Cherokee County** was established in 1839 and named to honor the Cherokee Indians who lived in the area. Murphy was named for Archibald De Bow Murphy, the "father of North Carolina public education."

The first court was held in a rented house until a brick courthouse was built in 1841. Torched by Union soldiers in 1865, the courthouse was immediately rebuilt using the same walls. A third courthouse was built in 1892 and burned in 1895. The fourth courthouse burned in 1926. The fifth courthouse, designed by James J. Baldwin, architect, and constructed by James Fanning, builder, was completed in 1926 at a cost of $256,000. This courthouse was built of marble and is purported to be the only all-marble fireproof courthouse in the state. An additional "rock gym" was built in 1974 to house a gymnasium and juvenile judicial offices. A jail is attached by a bridge to the courthouse. A museum is located adjacent to the courthouse.

The magistrate's office is in the town of Andrews. The Cherokee County Courthouse is on the *National Register of Historic Places.*

Cherokee County is in the Great Smoky Mountains. The Valley and Hiwassee Rivers are principle waterways. Lake Hiwassee was formed by the Hiwassee and Appalachia Dams. The area is home to the endangered barred owl. Hernando de Soto, the Spanish explorer, is said to have passed through the valley in 1540.

Census: 1950—18,294; 1995—21,865
Per capita income: $12,824
Land area: 454 square miles; elev. 1,535 ft.
Of Interest: Schools—Tri-County Community College in Murphy. Cultural Treasure—The John C. Campbell Folk School.

 **Chowan County** was established in the 1670s from the colonial county of Albemarle and named for an Algonquian Indian word *Sorwan* meaning "South" or "South Country." Edenton was incorporated in 1722 and named for Governor Charles Eden.

Under British rule, Edenton served as the capital of the Province of North Carolina and had a courthouse as early as 1718. The "tobacco barn," as it was described, was replaced in 1767 with the present Georgian courthouse. Large office buildings for judicial functions have been built in recent years. Cannons were placed in front of the courthouse in 1777, then dumped in the river so that the British would not get them. Several have been retrieved and are in place at the water's edge on the lawn in front of the courthouse. Chowan County Courthouse is a National Historic Landmark.

Chowan County, the smallest of North Carolina's one hundred counties, is located on the Chowan River and the Albemarle Sound. Edenton was a prosperous and busy port during the eighteenth and nineteenth centuries and claims to be "the prettiest town in the South." Twenty-three historic homes, many listed on the *National Register of Historic Places*, date from the eighteenth century.

> **Census:** 1950—12,540; 1995—14,064
> **Per capita income:** $15,679
> **Land area:** 180 square miles; elev. 16 ft.
> **Of Interest:** National Historic Landmarks—Cupola House, the Hayes Plantation, and Edenton (along with the Courthouse). Cultural Treasure—Chowan Museum. State Historic Sites—Courthouse, Cupola House (*ca*1725), Barker House (1782), and Somerset Place (1830). Produce—Peanuts are a major crop.

Clay County was established in 1861 and named for Henry Clay of Kentucky. Hayesville was named for George W. Hayes, a legislator who helped form the county.

Clay County's first courthouse, a wooden building, burned in 1870. The Masonic Hall and the Presbyterian Church served until a brick courthouse was built in 1889. The Clay County Courthouse is listed on the *National Register of Historic Places*.

Clay County is located in the scenic mountains of North Carolina. Major attractions are the Nantahala National Forest and the Chatuge Lake, created by a dam on the Hiwassee River. The Appalachian Trail passes through the county.

Census: 1950—6,006; 1995—7,743
Per capita income: $13,591
Land area: 213 square miles; elev. 1,893 ft.
Of Interest: Cultural Treasure—Clay County Art and Cultural Center. Produce—tobacco, corn, soybeans, dairy and beef cattle, and chickens. Industry—electrical equipment, non-electrical machinery, and apparel.

Clay County Seat—Hayesville, North Carolina 28904   *33*

Cleveland County was established in 1841 and named for Colonel Benjamin Cleveland, one of the heroes of the Battle of Kings Mountain in the Revolution. Shelby was incorporated in 1843 and named for Colonel Isaac Shelby, Revolutionary War hero.

Cleveland County's first permanent courthouse was built of logs in 1842. Brick courthouses were built in 1874 and 1907. The present courthouse was built in 1974. The 1907 courthouse is a museum and meeting hall and is on the *National Register of Historic Places*.

The Broad River passes through the southwestern part of the county. Crowder's Mountain State Park is noted for ninety species of birds that nest there.

Census: 1950—64,357; 1995—89,138
Per capita income: $16,514
Land area: 466 square miles; elev. 853 ft.
Of Interest: Schools—Gardner-Webb University in Boiling Springs. Cultural Treasure—Cleveland County Historical Museum. Produce—cotton, eggs, and cattle. Industry—stone, clay, and glass products, textiles, chemicals, printing, and transportation equipment. Mining—feldspar and lithium.

 ***Columbus County*** was established in 1808 from Bladen and Brunswick Counties and named for explorer and navigator Christopher Columbus. Whiteville was established in 1810 and named for John White, first governor of colonial Virginia, part of which later became North Carolina.

Columbus County's first courthouse was built of wood in Whiteville in 1809 and replaced by a brick building in 1852. In 1913 a fireproof courthouse was built at a cost of $50,000; Joseph L. Leitner was the architect. This courthouse is on the *National Register of Historic Places.* In 1995 the courthouse became the setting for a movie. The name over the front entrance was changed from Columbus to Greenville County, and a brick facade, built on the western side of the building, was set ablaze. The Columbus County name remained unchanged on the eastern side.

Columbus County, the second largest county in the state, is a rural county with large areas of swamp land. The Lumber, the Waccamaw, and the Cape Fear Rivers border the county on the west and east. Waccamaw Lake is the site of a state park.

Census: 1950—50,621; 1995—51,195
Per capita income: $15,301
Land area: 939 square miles; elev. 59 ft.
Of Interest: Schools—Southeastern Community College in Whiteville. Produce—corn, tobacco, and hogs. Industry—textiles, apparel, wood, and paper products.

Craven County was established in 1712 and named for Lord Proprietor William Lord Craven. New Bern was established in 1723 and named for Bern, Switzerland, by early settlers who were Swiss and German. New Bern was, for a time, the capital of North Carolina.

The first courthouse was erected on Craven Street. The second, at the intersection of Broad and Middle, was completed in 1764 and was the site, in 1785, of a famous case which separated legislative from judicial powers. Chief Justice John Marshall cited this case in establishing judicial review as a fundamental principle of American law. This courthouse was destroyed by fire in 1861, and court was held in private buildings for some twenty years. The current courthouse was completed in 1883 and remodeled in 1958. The New Bern Historic District is on the *National Register of Historic Places.*

The Neuse and Trent Rivers flow through Craven County and are bordered by extensive forests. The Croatan National Forest boasts exotic wildlife including the Venus flytrap, squawroot, deer, black bear, red woodpecker, eagle, and osprey. The county is home to Cherry Point, the largest U.S. Marine Corps air station.

Census: 1950—48,823; 1995—86,004
Per capita income: $16,979
Land area: 725 square miles; elev. 12 ft.
Of Interest: Schools—Craven Community College in New Bern. Tourist Attractions—Tryon Palace, once home of the British Royal Governor William Tryon. Major events held at Tryon Palace include historic drama tours and Christmas celebrations. Historic Sites—the Civil War Museum, Fireman's Museum, Academy Museum, Attmore-Oliver House, Bank of Arts, Bellair Plantation, and the New Bern Trolley.

Craven County Seat—New Bern, North Carolina 28560   37

Cumberland County was estab-
lished in 1754 from Bladen County and named for William Augustus, Duke of Cumberland, second son of King George II of England, who, in 1746, defeated the Highlanders of Scotland, many of whom came to settle in the county. Fayetteville was named in honor of the Marquis de Lafayette, who fought with American revolutionaries in the War for Independence.

Cumberland County has had six courthouses. The first was built in 1754 in Linden. The second, in 1778 in Campbellton, whose name was later changed to Fayetteville; the third, in 1790; the fourth, in 1893; the fifth, in 1926. The present sixth courthouse is part of a large county government complex built in 1978; Harry Barton was the architect.

The Cape Fear River, Little River, and South River run through the county. Fort Bragg Military Reservation occupies a large area of the county and extends into Hoke County.

Census: 1950—96,006; 1995—294,178
Per capita income: $16,403
Land area: 661 square miles; elev. 107 ft.
Of Interest: Schools—Fayetteville State University and Methodist College in Fayetteville. National Historic Landmark—Market House in Fayetteville. Points of Interest—St. John's Episcopal Church, Old Cool Springs, Kyle House, and Old Flour Mill. Babe Ruth hit his first home run and acquired his nickname in Fayetteville.

Cumberland County Seat—Fayetteville, North Carolina 28301 39

 **Currituck County** was formed around 1670 as a precinct of colonial Albemarle County and gets its name from an Indian word, *Coratank*, meaning "wild geese." The county seat, Currituck, was, until recently, called "Currituck Courthouse."

In 1723 a courthouse was built in Currituck Courthouse, an unincorporated village near the shores of Currituck Sound, which separates the mainland from the Outer Banks. The second courthouse was built in 1842 and replaced by the present building in 1869. A second floor was added in 1897 and a rear wing in 1952. The Currituck County Courthouse is on the *National Register of Historic Places*.

The county occupies the northeast corner of the state and is surrounded by the North River, Albemarle Sound, Currituck Sound, and the Atlantic Ocean. The Intracoastal Waterway cuts through the county. The county has many islands, including Mackay Island National Wildlife Refuge. A ferry connects Currituck to Knott's Island. Fishing for walleye is a lively sport.

Census: 1950—6,201; 1995—15,807
Per capita income: $15,899
Land area: 273 square miles; elev. 8 ft.
Of Interest: Produce—soybeans, corn, wheat, potatoes, peaches, and hogs.

Dare County was established in 1871–1872 from Currituck, Tyrrell, and Hyde Counties and named for Virginia Dare, the first child of English parents in America. Manteo, which was named for an Indian chief, is on Roanoke Island, and is reached by a bridge across Croatan Sound from the west. The highway bridge across Roanoke Sound connects Roanoke Island to Nags Head and the Outer Banks to the east.

The first courthouse was built of cypress wood in 1873. A brick courthouse, costing approximately $16,500, was built in 1904 and still serves the county.

In 1903 Orville and Wilbur Wright made their first flight of 120 feet on Kill Devil sand dunes, four miles south of Kitty Hawk. The Wright Brothers National Museum houses their glider and early aeroplane.

Census: 1950—5,405; 1995—25,693
Per capita income: $17,625
Land area: 388 square miles; elev. 12 ft.
Of Interest: State Historic Site—The *Elizabeth II* sailing ship, representing Sir Walter Raleigh's Roanoke Voyages. Of Interest—Elizabethan Gardens on Roanoke Island, *Lost Colony* outdoor drama on the Outer Banks, and North Carolina Aquarium. Summer residents, tourists, timber, and shellfish are the main sources of income. Tourist Attractions—National Seashore, Fort Raleigh National Historic Site, and Jockey's Ridge State Park.

Davidson County was established in 1822 and named for William Lee Davidson, Revolutionary War hero. Davidson College and Davidson County, Tennessee, are also named for William Lee Davidson. Lexington was named for the Revolutionary Battle of Lexington, Massachusetts.

A brick courthouse, built in 1825, included a jail, stocks, and adjacent whipping post. This courthouse burned and was replaced in 1850. Before the Civil War, slaves were exhibited by standing them on large boulders placed at each side of the courthouse entrance. Union soldiers burned this courthouse, but it was rebuilt in 1868 using the same walls. In 1918 the granite blocks were covered with stucco. A new courthouse was built in 1959; architects were Echols-Sparger and Associates. The 1868 courthouse is on the *National Register of Historic Places*.

The Yadkin River and High Rock Lake are in the western part of the county; Uwharrie National Forest is in the south. Boone's Cave State Park is on Highway 150 southwest of Lexington.

Census: 1950—62,244; 1995—136,413
Per capita income: $17,153
Land area: 548 square miles; elev. 810 ft.
Of Interest: Schools—Davidson County Community College in Lexington. Produce—beef cattle, chickens, hogs, tobacco, wheat, corn, and soybeans. Industry—furniture and wood products, machinery and electrical equipment, paper and printing, food processing, fabricated metals, stone, clay, glass, rubber, plastics, and leather products.

Davidson County Seat—Lexington, North Carolina 28036   43

 **Davie County** was established in 1836 from Rowan County and named for William Richardson Davie, Revolutionary War hero, a founder of the University of North Carolina, governor of North Carolina, minister to France, and member of the Federal Convention of 1787. Mocksville was named for the Mock family.

Court was first held in the Methodist Church in Mocksville until 1839, when the first courthouse was built. In 1866 an ordinance was passed to assess a fine of $25 to "horsemen who galloped down the courthouse corridor." A second courthouse, built in 1909, was seriously damaged by fire in 1916; however, it was possible to repair and renovate it. This old courthouse was later demolished, and the present courthouse was constructed when the street was widened in 1922. The courthouse was renovated in 1971 and an annex constructed. The Davie County Courthouse is on the *National Register of Historic Places.*

The Yadkin and the South Yadkin Rivers join to form the south and eastern borders of the county. In 1753 Lord Granville granted 640 acres on Bear Creek to Squire Boone who sold it to his son Daniel Boone in 1759.

Census: 1950—15,420; 1995—29,784
Per capita income: $21,305
Land area: 264 square miles; elev. 866 ft.
Of Interest: National Historic Landmarks—Cooleemee and the Hinton Rowan Helper House in Mocksville. Produce—corn, wheat, tobacco, soybeans, cotton, chickens, and beef and dairy cattle.

44   *Davie County Seat—Mocksville, North Carolina 27028*

Duplin County was established in
1749 and named for George Henry Hay, Lord
Duplin, a member of the Board of Trade and
Plantations. Kenansville was named for the Kenan family, whose elegant home still stands. James Kenan was a member of the Provincial Congress, Revolutionary leader, brigadier general in the militia, and a trustee of the University of North Carolina.

The first courthouse was built in 1775 three miles from Warsaw. A second courthouse was built in 1784 at James Tavern, one mile from Kenansville. The town of Kenansville was laid out in 1816 and a courthouse was built. Remodeled in 1842, it served until the present courthouse was built in 1911. In 1959 a two-story addition was attached, and in the 1970s the courthouse was remodeled with a large jail added. The courthouse is in the Kenansville Historic District on the *National Register of Historic Places*.

Duplin County is located in the Cape Fear River valley. A

Confederate arms factory in Kenansville was destroyed on July 4, 1863, by Federal cavalry.

Census: 1950—41,074; 1995—42,792
Per capita income: $17,118
Land area: 822 square miles: elev. 127 ft.
Of Interest: Schools—James Sprunt Community College in Kenansville. Tourist Attractions—Kenan Plantation House, Rose Hill Winery, and Duplin County Cowan Museum. The Albertson Fox Hunt is held yearly on George Washington's birthday. The world's largest frying pan is in Rose Hill, and the Kenansville Historic District contains sixteen structures listed on the *National Register of Historic Places*.

Duplin County Seat—Kenansville, North Carolina 28349

Durham County was established

in 1881 and named for Dr. Bartholomew Durham, owner of the land which included the railway station and the central part of the city. The county seat was also named Durham.

The first brick courthouse was built in 1885. A second courthouse, described as one of the finest in the state, was built in 1916 at a cost of $250,000; the designer was Milbury and Heister. The current courthouse, built in the 1970s and 80s, is a seven-story building of steel frame with white precast concrete panels; two-story glass walls frame the doorways. The old and new courthouses are joined.

Durham County is located in the Piedmont foothills and is part of the Research Triangle. While the inner city shows evidence of decline, Duke University, with the Duke Chapel and its 210-foot tower and 50-bell carillon, the Medical Center, and the Duke University Museum of Art, dominate the landscape on the edge of the city. Processing tobacco became a major industry during the Civil War after a farmer named Washington Duke noticed Union

soldiers "going for" his Bright Leaf tobacco. By 1874 the next generation of Dukes (Buck and Ben) were mass-producing cigarettes.

Census: 1950—101,639; 1995—192,961
Per capita income: $21,547
Land area: 299 square miles; elev. 400 ft.
Of Interest: Schools—Duke University, Durham Technical Community College, and N.C. Central University. National Historic Landmarks—Duke Homestead and Tobacco Factory, North Carolina Mutual Life Insurance Company (Mechanics & Farmers Bank), and W. T. Blackwell and Company Tobacco Factory. Of Interest—Bennett Place Historic Site (where the largest surrender of the Civil War took place), Patterson's Mill Country Store, West Point on the Eno, Sarah P. Duke Gardens, the Primate Center, the Museum of Life and Science, Hayti Heritage Center, and the Royal Center for the Arts.

Edgecombe County was established in 1741 from Bertie County and named for Baron Richard Edgecombe, a Lord of the Treasury. Tarboro, established in 1760, became the county seat in 1764. In the Indian Tuscarora language, *Tarboro* means "town of the dark waters."

Edgecombe County has had four courthouses. The first, of wood, was constructed in 1735. A second wooden courthouse was built in 1790. A third courthouse was built in 1850 and remodeled in 1912. A large brick annex was built at the rear of the courthouse in 1953. The fourth and current courthouse was built in 1965 by Taylor and Crabtree of Nashville, Tennessee, architects, and T. A. Loving, contractor. A reflecting pool and park surround the courthouse.

Census: 1950—51,639; 1995—56,669
Per capita income: $15,432
Land area: 511 square miles; elev. 54 ft.
Of Interest: Schools—Edgecombe Community College in Tarboro. National Historic Landmark—Coolmore. Historic Attractions—Tarboro Historical District, Hobson Pittman (poet, painter) Memorial Gallery, and the Historic Recreational Trail. Main Street is a project of the National Trust for Historic Preservation. Produce—tobacco, peanuts, corn, cotton, and hogs. Industry—non-electrical machinery, chemicals, instruments, and primary metals.

Forsyth County was established
in 1849 and named for Colonel Benjamin Forsyth, who was killed in the War of 1812. The Winston of Winston-Salem was named for Revolutionary Army Colonel Joseph Winston. The independent Moravian town of Salem (meaning "peace") was settled in 1766 and joined with Winston in 1913 to create the city of Winston-Salem.

The first courthouse, which was built in Germantown in 1850, had a cupola and a 300-pound bell. In 1895 a new courthouse, said to resemble a Russian cathedral, was built and is on the *National Register of Historic Places*. This courthouse was remodeled in 1927 and expanded in 1959–1960. A new courthouse was completed in 1975. This Forsyth County Hall of Justice was designed by Fred W. Butner Jr., architect, and constructed by H. L. Coble Construction Company.

Census: 1950—146,135; 1995—280,328
Per capita income: $23,579
Land area: 424 square miles; elev. 858 ft.
Of Interest: Schools—Salem College, Wake Forest University, Winston-Salem State University, Forsyth Technical Community College, and N.C. School of the Arts. National Historic Landmarks—Old Salem, Salem Tavern, and Single Brothers House in Winston-Salem. Old Salem is "A Living History Museum" containing the German-speaking Moravian Church, its cemetery, and town. Points of Interest—Nature Science Center, Bethabara, Tanglewood Park, Southeastern Center for Contemporary Art, African art at Reynolds House, R. J. Reynolds Tobacco Company, and Yadkin River Recreation Area.

Forsyth County Seat—Winston-Salem, North Carolina 27100   49

 *Franklin County* was established in 1779 and named for Benjamin Franklin, American statesman and philosopher. Louisburg was named for the Canadian city-fort captured from France in 1757.

The first courthouse was built in 1781; the log structure was later weatherboarded and served until 1850. The present courthouse was built in 1850 of brick and was remodeled 1936–1937. It was again renovated and enlarged in 1968; Harry J. Harles was the architect and J. M. Thompson was the general contractor. In 1872, Daniel G. Fowler, a famous orator and later governor, delivered a eulogy on the Confederacy and the Old South to a packed audience in the courthouse.

Franklin County is located in the Tar River valley. The county annually hosts the National Whistlers Convention during the last two weeks of April.

Census: 1950—31,341; 1995—41,588
Per capita income: $14,858
Land area: 494 square miles; elev. 280 ft.
Of Interest: Perry's Mill Pond, which was built in 1778 near Dunn. The county is being reforested with loblolly pine. Produce—tobacco, wheat, corn, soybeans, hogs, and beef cattle. Industry—apparel manufacturing.

Gaston County was established in 1864. Both the county and the county seat were named for William Gaston, member of Congress and judge of the Supreme Court of North Carolina. Dallas was the county seat until 1909.

The first courthouse was built of logs in Dallas in 1847. A brick structure was erected in 1848 and burned in 1874. The walls were left standing and the courthouse was rebuilt using the same walls. In 1909, after the merchants of Gastonia pledged $43,000 for the new courthouse in Gastonia and the county commission raised $10,000 for the land, the county seat was moved by popular vote to Gastonia. The courthouse and jail were constructed for approximately $60,000; Frank P. Milburn was the architect. Gaston County Courthouse is on the *National Register of Historic Places*.

The eastern border of the county is formed by the Catawba River, Mountain Island Lake, and Henry River.

Census: 1950—110,836; 1995—178,478
Per capita income: $17,602
Land area: 352 square miles; elev. 825 ft.
Of Interest: Schools—Belmont Abbey College in Belmont, Gaston College in South Dallas, and N.C. Center for Applied Textile Technology in Belmont. Natural Heritage Site—Crowder's Mountain State Park. King's Mountain National Military Park commemorates a famous Revolutionary battle. Cultural Treasure—Schiele Museum of Natural History and Planetarium. Produce—wheat, corn, peanuts, soybeans, and cotton. Industry—textiles, non-electrical machinery, and transportation equipment. Mining—lithium.

Gates County was established in

1779. Both the county and the county seat were named for General Horatio Gates who commanded the Revolutionary Army at the surrender of the British at Saratoga, New York.

The first courthouse was built in 1780. A second courthouse was built in 1834–1836. In 1904 the original brick was covered with stucco. An addition and jail were added to the rear in 1940. This courthouse is on the *National Register of Historic Places*. A new courthouse was built in 1976.

Gates County is a largely agricultural county. The Great Dismal Swamp occupies much of the eastern part of the county. The Merchants Millpond State Park is a popular recreational facility.

Census: 1950—9,555; 1995—9,761
Per capita income: $14,855
Land area: 350 square miles; elev. 40 ft.
Of Interest: Produce—peanuts, corn, soybeans, and hogs.

Gates County Seat—Gatesville, North Carolina 27938   53

 *Graham County* was established in 1872 from Cherokee County and named for William A. Graham, Confederate senator, secretary of the Navy, North Carolina governor, and United States senator. Robbinsville was named for a local family.

The first county courthouse was built in Rhea Hill in 1873; then moved and rebuilt in Robbinsville in 1874. A third courthouse was built in 1886. The present courthouse was built in 1942. Each step to the entrance of the courthouse bears the name of someone from the county who was killed in action in U.S. military service.

The Cherokee Indian Chief Junaluska (*ca*1776–1868) and his wife are buried in a memorial park in Robbinsville. Chief Junaluska is credited with saving the life of General Andrew Jackson at the battle of Horse Shoe Bend during the Creek War of 1814. For his heroism, Junaluska was awarded U.S. citizenship and given land.

Robbinsville lies within the Nantahala National Forest and encompasses the Joyce Kilmer (author of "Trees" and other poems) Memorial Forest.

Census: 1950—6,886; 1995—7,478
Per capita income: $11,930
Land area: 289 square miles; elev. 2,150 ft.
Of Interest: Natural Heritage Site—Slickrock Wilderness. Signs posted on the hiking trails warn hikers of bears. The Santeetlah Wildlife Management Area is heavily wooded. The Santeetlah Lake is above the dam on the Little Tennessee River. Fontana Lake, below the dam, borders the Great Smoky Mountains. White-water rafting is a popular sport. The Appalachian Trail passes through the county. Industry—furniture manufacturing.

Granville County was established in 1746 and named for John Carteret, Earl of Granville, who owned the Granville District. He was prime minister under George II and one of the Lord Proprietors of the colony. Oxford was probably named for Oxford, England.

The first courthouse was built in Harrisburg. The second courthouse was built in 1820 in Oxford. A third courthouse was built in 1837. The fourth courthouse was built in 1839 of brick and is still in use, with enlargements in 1891 and an annex added in 1937. The courthouse was renovated and restored in 1987–1989. Surapon Sujjavanich was the architect; Light's General Construction, Inc., the contractor. The Granville Courthouse is on the *National Register of Historic Places*.

Granville County is perched in the Piedmont section; the Tar River runs through it. Buggs Island Lake is part of the John H. Kerr Reservoir on the border with Virginia. Camp Butner Military Reservation is in the southwest corner of the county.

Census: 1950—31,793; 1995—41,088
Per capita income: $15,191
Land area: 543 square miles; elev. 476 ft.
Of Interest: Produce—Tobacco is the county's major product.

Granville County Seat—Oxford, North Carolina 27565

 **Greene County** was established in 1799 and named for General Nathanael Greene, one of the outstanding soldiers of the Revolutionary War. The county was first named for James Glasgow, but changed to Greene when Glasgow was found to be involved in land frauds. In 1811 Snow Hill was established as the county seat.

The first wooden courthouse was built in 1800. This courthouse was replaced by a brick building in 1848 and was burned by the sheriff in 1876. The courthouse was promptly rebuilt. In 1939 the Federal Emergency Administration of Public Works provided $107,800 for a new courthouse and jail. Thomas B. Herman was the architect. The Greene County Courthouse is on the *National Register of Historic Places*.

Greene County is almost completely rural, with no large towns or cities. The courthouse is the largest structure in the county. Many small creeks and streams drain into the Neuse River southeast of the county; marshlands abound. The county is part of the coastal plain.

Census: 1950—18,024; 1995—16,760
Per capita income: $16,287
Land area: 269 square miles; elev. 74 ft.
Of Interest: Produce—hogs. The county is rural with no major industries.

Guilford County was established

in 1771 and named for Francis North, Earl of Guilford, father of Lord North, the prime minister under King George III. Greensboro was named in honor of General Nathanael Greene.

Guilford County has had nine courthouses. The first was built in 1773 at Guilford Courthouse (name later changed to Martinsville); the second, in 1788. In 1807 the county seat was moved to Greensboro, and a third courthouse was completed in 1809. The fourth courthouse was built in 1820; a fifth, in 1830; and a sixth, in 1858, burned in 1872. The seventh courthouse was built in 1873, demolished in 1919, and the eighth courthouse was completed in 1920. In 1974 this courthouse became part of a county government complex when combined with a modern ninth courthouse. The architects were Eduardo Catalano and Peter Sugar of Cambridge, Massachusetts; McMinn, Norfleet, and Wicker of Greensboro were associate architects. The 1920 courthouse is on the *National Register of Historic Places*.

Guilford Courthouse is a National Military Park where in 1781 a quarter of General Cornwallis's forces were cut down by troops under the command of General Greene. This major defeat influenced the final American victory at Yorktown.

Census: 1950—191,057; 1995—372,317
Per capita income: $22,530
Land area: 651 square miles; elev. 838 ft.
Of Interest: Schools—(in Greensboro) Bennett College, Guilford College, Greensboro College, N.C. Agricultural and Technical State University, and UNC-Greensboro. Also (in High Point) High Point University. National Historic Landmark—Blandwood Mansion & Carriage House. Industry—furniture, textiles, brick, and fabricated metal products. Produce—tobacco, poultry, and dairy products.

Halifax County was established in 1758 and named for George Montagu, Earl of Halifax. The county seat, also named Halifax, was founded in 1760.

Halifax has had four court-houses. The first courthouse was built in 1759; the second in 1847; the third in 1910. In 1965 an addition enlarged the courthouse. The fourth, a large courthouse complex built on expansive grounds on the edge of the town, was completed in 1987. The 1910 courthouse is on the *National Register of Historic Places*.

Halifax County is in the Roanoke River valley, where, historically, there were many large plantations. Historic Halifax has a number of homes built in the 1700s on the banks of the Roanoke River. On April 12, 1776, Halifax County became the first colony to vote for independence when the Provincial Congress adopted the Halifax Resolve that led to the Declaration of Independence signed on July 4, 1776, at Philadelphia. The outdoor drama *First for Freedom* is a popular annual July 4 event in Halifax. Medoc Mountain State Park and the Little Fishing Creek, famous for various sport fish, are popular for recreation. Roanoke Rapids Lake is on the northern border of the county. Stock car racing is held at Champion Raceway near Roanoke Rapids.

Census: 1950—58,377; 1995—57,183
Per capita income: $14,587
Land area: 722 square miles; elev. 135 ft.
Of Interest: Schools—Halifax Community College in Weldon. Produce—tobacco, corn, peanuts, and soybeans. Industry—plastic, rubber, leather goods, and stone/glass/clay goods.

Harnett County was established in 1855 and named for Cornelius Harnett, a Revolutionary patriot from Cape Fear, hero of the battle of Moore's Creek, and an author of the Halifax Resolve of April 1776 (see Halifax County). He was also a delegate to the Continental Congress and president of the Provincial Council. Lillington was named for Revolutionary General Alexander Lillington. The county seat was moved to Lillington in 1866.

Harnett County's courts were held in Toomer at the Summerville Academy until 1866 when a wooden courthouse was built in Lillington. This courthouse was burned by an arsonist in 1892 and a second courthouse was also burned in 1894. A brick courthouse was built in 1898. In 1959 the present courthouse was constructed; Frank B. Simpson was the architect.

The Cape Fear River runs through the county.

Census: 1950—47,605; 1995—76,959
Per capita income: $14,525
Land area: 627 square miles; elev. 325 ft.
Of Interest: Schools—Campbell University in Buies Creek with its noted Keith Hills Golf Course. Points of Interest—Raven Rock State Park, Averysboro Battleground (site of a Confederate attack in 1865 on General Sherman's Army), and Barbecue Presbyterian Church, built by Scottish Highlanders in 1757. Interesting Facts— Harnett Arts Council is the umbrella for the Harnett Regional Theater, Harnett Art Guild, Helena Wade Music Club, and the Cape Fear Writers Guild. Produce—tobacco, corn, soybeans, sweet potatoes, and livestock, including hogs.

Haywood County was established in 1808 and named for John Haywood, treasurer of North Carolina. Waynesville was named for General Anthony Wayne, Revolutionary War hero.

The first courts were held at Mount Prospect. Waynesville became the county seat in 1811 and the courthouse was built in 1812. This building was replaced by a brick courthouse in 1844. A third courthouse was built in 1884. In 1931 the building was condemned and bonds were issued for $230,000 to finance the present courthouse, completed in 1932. This courthouse is on the *National Register of Historic Places.*

The Pigeon River drains the valley, and many surrounding peaks are over 5,000 feet.

Census: 1950—37,631; 1995—49,962
Per capita income: $16,217
Land area: 543 square miles; elev. 2,635 ft.
Of Interest: Schools—Haywood Community College in Clyde. Natural Heritage Sites—Great Smoky Mountains National Park (which runs through Haywood and Swain Counties), Graveyard Fields, and Mount Hardy. Cultural Treasure—Museum of North Carolina Handicrafts. Scenic Destinations—Blue Ridge Parkway, Pisgah National Forest, and the Sherwood Wildlife Management Area. Tourist Attractions—Maggie Valley, "Ghost Town in the Sky." The Harmon Den exit on Interstate 40 leads to Max Patch, a great bald on the Appalachian Trail with a spectacular view of Tennessee and North Carolina.

Haywood County Seat—Waynesville, North Carolina 28786   61

Henderson County was established in 1838. Both the county and the county seat, Hendersonville, were named for Leonard Henderson, Chief Justice of the Supreme Court of North Carolina.

The county seat was laid out and the first courthouse was built in 1840. This wooden courthouse was replaced in 1845 with a brick courthouse. In 1904 architect R. S. Smith, who had worked on the Biltmore Village, designed and built an impressive courthouse with a large golden dome on top of the cupola. A large county government complex, three blocks from the old courthouse, was dedicated in 1995. The old courthouse is on the *National Register of Historic Places* and is used for administrative and sheriff's offices.

Henderson County is a mountainous county, where forests cover 60 percent of the land. Pisgah National Forest and the Blue Ridge Parkway are in the northern section, a summer resort area.

Census: 1950—30,921; 1995—76,262
Per capita income: $19,335
Land area: 382 square miles; elev. 2,146 ft.
Of Interest: National Historic Landmark—Carl Sandburg House in Flat Rock is owned by the U.S. Government. Cultural Treasures—Johnson Farm and Historic Flat Rock. Natural Historic Site—Green River Gorge runs through Henderson and Polk Counties.

 ***Hertford County*** was established in 1759 and named for Francis Seymour Conway, Earl and later Marquis of Hertford, a Lord of the Bed Chamber, Knight of the Garter, and a brother of a member of Parliament who favored repeal of the Stamp Act. Winton was named for Benjamin Wynn (or "Wynnton").

The first court was held at Cotton's Ferry on the south bank of the Chowan River. Winton was established as the county seat in 1766. The date of the building of the first courthouse in Winton is uncertain; however, in 1830 the courthouse was torched by an arsonist. In 1862, the next courthouse was burned along with the town, the first entire town to be burned during the Civil War. A new courthouse, built in 1875 and remodeled in 1905, was torn down in 1956 in order to build the current courthouse. This courthouse cost $450,000; John J. Rowland was the architect.

The Chowan River forms the eastern border and large swamps cover much of this lowland county.

> **Census:** 1950—21,453; 1995—22,445
> **Per capita income:** $13,246
> **Land area:** 356 square miles; elev. 45 ft.
> **Of Interest:** Schools—Roanoke-Chowan Community College in Ahoskie and Chowan College in Murfreesboro. Produce—peanuts, corn, soybeans, and cotton. Cotton is no longer baled, but is compacted by machines to fit an eighteen-wheeler truck. The loads are then covered with plastic sheeting and left in the fields until hauled away.

 *Hoke County* was established in 1911 and named for Major General Robert F. Hoke of the Confederate Army. The name of the county seat, Raeford, is from the last syllables of J. A. MacRae and A. A. Williford, the men who incorporated the town in 1901.

The first three terms of the court were held in the Raeford High School auditorium. The courthouse cost $57,000, was completed in 1912, and is on the *National Register of Historic Places*. The architect was the firm of Milburn and Heister of Washington, D.C.

Hoke County is a sparsely settled, rural county lying in the Lumber River valley; 60 percent of the land is forested. Much of the northern part of the county is occupied by Fort Bragg Military Reservation.

Census: 1950—15,756; 1995—27,306
Per capita income: $11,921
Land area: 414 square miles; elev. 262 ft.
Of Interest: Produce—turkeys, tobacco, soybeans, corn, and hogs.

Hoke County Seat—Raeford, North Carolina 28376

Hyde County was established in 1705 from Bath County and was known as Wickham County until 1712. The county was named for Edward Hyde, governor of North Carolina, who died that same year. Swan Quarter was named for the swans that migrate yearly to Lake Mattamuskett.

Courts were held in Bath until 1729. A courthouse, built in 1729 in Woodstock on the Pungo River, burned in 1789. In 1790 the county seat moved to Bell's Bay (or Jasper's Creek). After one year a county courthouse was built on German Bernard's land and was named German-town. In 1820 this courthouse was sold and a new courthouse was built at Lake Landing on the southeastern side of Lake Mattamuskett. In 1836 Zacheriah Gibbs sold land to the county at Swan Quarter where the present county seat was established; a courthouse was built in 1850, replaced in 1878, and renovated in 1909 and in 1964. The Hyde County Courthouse is on the *National Register of Historic Places.*

Hyde County is bordered by Pamlico Sound, Ocracoke Island, the Atlantic Ocean, the Pungo River, and the Alligator River. Lake Mattamuskett, a wildlife refuge since 1934, is the largest lake in the state.

Census: 1950—6,479; 1995—5,204
Per capita income: $15,142
Land area: 1,364 square miles; elev. 10 ft.
Of Interest: National Historic Landmark—U.S.S. *Monitor,* anchored off Cape Hatteras. Cape Hatteras National Seashore is partly in the county. A toll ferry connects Swan Quarter and Ocracoke Island. Produce—shellfish, corn, and soybeans. Industry—lumber.

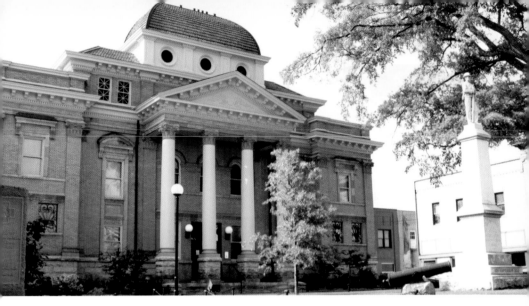

 *Iredell County* was established in 1788 and named for James Iredell, an advocate for the adoption of the Federal Constitution. In 1790, Iredell was appointed by President George Washington to the Supreme Court.

The 1789 log cabin courthouse in Statesville was replaced with a brick courthouse in 1819, which was destroyed by fire in 1854. The third courthouse was completed in 1856 and a fourth in 1899. A rear wing was added in 1940. In 1972 a Hall of Justice, designed by Hayden, Wheeler, and Schwend Architects, was built. The 1899 courthouse is on the *National Register of Historic Places*.

In 1760, Cherokees raided Fort Dobbs and were defeated by Hugh Waddell and his rangers, which extended the western frontier by fifty miles.

Census: 1950—56,303; 1995—103,564
Per capita income: $18,297
Land area: 591 square miles; elev. 925 ft.
Of Interest: Schools—Mitchell Community College in Statesville. Produce—beef production, milk, hogs, chickens, tobacco, and soybeans. Industry—precision instruments, fabricated metals, furniture, paper, stone, clay, and glass products.

Iredell County Seat—Statesville, North Carolina 28677   67

 **Jackson County** was established in 1851 and named for Andrew Jackson, "Old Hickory," the hero of the Battle of New Orleans against the British in the War of 1812 and the seventh president of the United States.

The first courthouse was built in 1855 in Webster (named for Daniel Webster). In the 1913 election the county seat was moved to Sylva, a popular tourist center along Scott Creek. In 1914 this gem of a courthouse (photo above), designed by the architects Smith and Carrier of Asheville, was built for $30,000. The courthouse was renovated in 1933–1934 with Federal Emergency Relief Funds and is on the *National Register of Historic Places*. From U.S. Highway 23 the white-painted building offers a vivid picture through an opening in the forest and is one of the most dramatically-sited buildings in the state. It is now the sheriff's office (on the first floor); the second floor can be used for courtrooms. In 1994 a more modern and functional Justice and Administration Center was built for $6 million on a site hidden from the highway.

The northern section of the county is a Cherokee Indian Reservation. The Nantahala Forest occupies much of the county. The Tuckasegee River flows through the county among many great peaks (4,000–6,000 feet). Thorpe Lake and Lake Sapphire, as well as the Tuckasegee River, are major recreational attractions.

Census: 1950—19,261; 1995—28,834
Per capita income: $14,740
Land area: 496 square miles; elev. 2,047 ft.
Of Interest: Schools—Southwestern Community College in Sylva and Western Carolina University in Cullowhee. Cultural Treasures—Whitewater Falls and the Mountain Heritage Center. Natural Heritage Sites—Chattooga River Gorge, Panthertown Valley, Rich, Balsam, and Whiteside Mountains. Tourist Attractions—Cashiers is a prominent resort community. Dillsboro is the home of the Great Smoky Mountain Railway. Points of Interest—Judaculla Rock, ancient pictographs, and Richland Balsam Overlook (highest point on the Blue Ridge Parkway—6,053 ft.). Lakes—Bear, Cedar Cliff, Thorpe, and Wolf. Products—tobacco, corn, wheat, and beef cattle. Industry—tourism, paper, apparel, and wood products.

Johnston County was established in 1746 and named for Gabriel Johnston, North Carolina governor from 1734–1754.

Smithfield was established as county seat in 1777 and named for John Smith on whose land the town was built.

The first courthouse was built in Clayton. In 1760 a second courthouse was built at Hinton's Quarter (now in Wake County). When Wake County was formed in 1771, court was held in John Smith's home near the Neuse River. In 1777 Smithfield was established, and a courthouse was built. In 1797 a courthouse was built on a new site. In 1921 this courthouse was replaced by the present courthouse. The Johnston County Courthouse is on the *National Register of Historic Places.*

The Neuse River flows through the county. The heavily-traveled Interstate highways 95 and 40 intersect in Johnston County.

Census: 1950—65,906; 1995—95,512
Per capita income: $17,450
Land area: 795 square miles; elev. 155 ft.
Of Interest: Schools—Johnston Community College in Smithfield. National Historic Landmark— Bentonville Battlefield Historic Site. Produce—tobacco, corn, and hogs.

Jones County was established in 1779 and named for Willie Jones, president of the Council of Safety during the Revolution.

Trenton was originally called Trent Bridge.

The first courthouse of wood was built in 1780. A second courthouse (construction date unknown) was burned in 1862 during a battle between Federal and Confederate troops. The third courthouse was completed in 1865. The fourth courthouse was completed in 1939 at a cost of $75,000 of Federal Works Progress Administration funds and $30,000 of bonds. The Jones County Courthouse is on the *National Register of Historic Places*.

Half of the Hoffman Forest, a North Carolina University research forest, is in the southern section of the county. The Croatan National Forest, 155,000 acres, provides a native habitat for alligators and a recreational area.

Census: 1950—11,004; 1995—9,528
Per capita income: $18,838
Land area: 467 square miles; elev. 28 ft.
Of Interest: Produce—soybeans, corn, and tobacco. Industry—textile and apparel.

Jones County Seat—Trenton, North Carolina 28585   71

 **Lee County** was established in 1907 from Moore and Chatham Counties and named for General Robert Edward Lee, commander of the Confederate armies. Sanford was named for a civil engineer who surveyed for the Seaboard Airline Railway.

The Lee County Courthouse was built in 1908; Charles McMillan was the architect. In 1954 a one-story brick wing was added. The courthouse is on the *National Register of Historic Places*.

Lee County is one of the smallest in the state and is mainly urban. Many Lee County residents commute daily to jobs in the Research Triangle area to the north.

Census: 1950—23,522; 1995—45,998
Per capita income: $19,699
Land area: 225 square miles; elev. 28 ft.
Of Interest: Schools—Central Carolina Community College in Sanford.

Lenoir County was established in 1791 and named for William Lenoir, a hero of the Revolutionary battle of Kings Mountain.

The county seat was first located in Dobbs County in 1764. In 1791, Kinston (formerly Kingstown) became the county seat of Lenoir County.

Lenoir County has had four courthouses. The first courthouse was built of wood in 1792. A brick courthouse, built in 1854, was burned in 1878 by a clerk of the court who also located and burned other court records; the arsonist was caught and imprisoned. A third courthouse was built in 1880. In 1939 the Federal Works Administration helped finance the building of the fourth courthouse. The Lenoir County Courthouse is on the *National Register of Historic Places*.

During the Civil War, the Confederate's ill-fated attempt to control the lower Neuse River and retake New Bern ended when the flat bottom, ironclad C.S.S. *Neuse* ran aground and was blown up to prevent capture by Federal troops.

Census: 1950—45,953; 1995—59,194
Per capita income: $17,333
Land area: 391 square miles; elev. 44 ft.
Of Interest: Schools—Lenoir Community College in Kinston. State Historic Site—In 1963, the wooden hull of the C.S.S. *Neuse* was raised and placed in the C.S.S. *Neuse* and Governor Caswell Memorial. Produce—tobacco, turkeys, and hogs. Industry—A large Dupont chemical plant is a major employer in the county.

Lenoir County Seat—Kinston, North Carolina 28755

Lincoln County was established in 1779 from Tryon County. Both county and county seat were named for General Benjamin Lincoln, a Revolutionary War hero, who was selected by George Washington to accept the surrender sword from British General Cornwallis at Yorktown.

The first court for Lincoln County met in 1783 in the home of Christian Mauney, nine miles from Lincolnton. About 1785 a log courthouse was erected in Lincolnton and replaced by a frame building in 1788. A third courthouse was built in 1810. In 1853 a brick and stone courthouse was constructed. The present courthouse, designed by architect James A. Slater of Raleigh, was completed in 1923. The War Memorial Plaza, built in 1970, graces the front of the courthouse. The Lincoln County Courthouse is on the *National Register of Historic Places*. Across the street is the Citizens' Center and county office building.

The county experienced a high rate of land conversion to urban use. Agriculture employs only 7.4 percent of the population.

> **Census:** 1950—27,459; 1995—55,673
> **Per capita income:** $16,915
> **Land area:** 308 square miles; elev. 860 ft.
> **Of Interest:** Cultural Treasure—Lincoln Cultural Center. Produce—wheat and soybeans. Industry—textiles.

McDowell County was established in 1842 and named for Colonel Joseph McDowell, an officer in the Revolution. Marion was named for Revolutionary War hero General Francis Marion.

The first courthouse was erected in 1844. In 1921 a new courthouse was constructed for $210,000; Erle G. Stillwell was the architect. This courthouse is on the *National Register of Historic Places*.

The northern half of the county is in the Pisgah National Forest. The Blue Ridge Parkway forms the northern border of the county.

Census: 1950—25,720; 1995—37,254
Per capita income: $14,740
Land area: 442 square miles; elev. 1,437 ft.
Of Interest: Schools—McDowell Technical Community College in Marion. Natural Heritage Site—Linville Caverns. Tourist Attractions—Little Switzerland and Linville Falls and gorges are scenic treats. Lake Tahoma and Lake James are recreational areas. Cultural Treasure—Carson House Museum in Pleasant Gardens, Mountain Gateway Museum in Old Fort, and Andrew's Geyser. Industry—furniture, fabricated metals, apparel, and food processing.

McDowell County Seat—Marion, North Carolina 28752   75

 **Macon County** was established in 1828 and named for Nathaniel Macon, speaker of the House of Representatives and president of the Constitutional Convention of 1835. Franklin was named for Benjamin Franklin. The town was built atop a sacred city of the Cherokee Indians.

In 1829 a brick courthouse was built in Franklin for $3,800. This courthouse was replaced in 1868. In 1881 a two-story brick courthouse was constructed for $8,900. The present courthouse, designed by Kyle C. Boone, was built in 1972.

Macon County lies within the Nantahala National Forest.

Census: 1950—16,174; 1995—26,204
Per capita income: $15,427
Land area: 517 square miles; elev. 2,113 ft.
Of Interest: Natural Historic Sites—Wayaha Bald & Fire Tower, Nantahala Bog, Chattooga River Gorge, Cullasaja River and Gorge, and Little Tennessee River Gorge. Tourist Attractions—Nantahala Lake, Dry Falls, Veil Falls, canoeing, and dig-your-own gem mines. Cultural Treasure—Scottish Tartan Museum. Industry—tourism. Produce—corn, apples, tobacco, dairy and beef cattle, chicken, and hogs.

Madison County was established

in 1851 from Buncombe County and named for James Madison, fourth president of the United States. Marshall, the county seat, originally named Lapland, was renamed to honor Chief Justice John Marshall of the U.S. Supreme Court.

Court was originally held in a log house at Jewel Hill (now Walnut) until Marshall was designated the county seat in 1853. A courthouse was completed in 1857. The present courthouse was built in 1907 for $30,000; Smith and Carrier were the architects. This courthouse design influenced the appearance of other courthouses in North Carolina through the 1930s. Marshall is on a narrow shelf of land overlooking the French Broad River. The Marshall County Courthouse, which is on the *National Register of Historic Places*, was featured in the highly acclaimed movie, "My Fellow Americans."

Much of Madison County is in the Pisgah National Forest. Large second-growth forests of hardwood, pine, and hemlock cover the mountains.

Census: 1950—20,522; 1995—17,770
Per capita income: $14,587
Land area: 456 square miles; elev. 1,650 ft.
Of Interest: Schools—Mars Hill College in Mars Hill. Cultural Treasure—Rural Life Museum. Natural Heritage Site—French Broad River and Rockie Bluff. The river drive could be developed to be a crown jewel of the area, offering bicycle and hiking trails, river rafting, and a parkway. A short passenger train ride between Marshall and Asheville (and possibly on to Black Mountain) would rival the Great Smoky Mountain Railway from Dillsboro to Bryson City as a major event for visitors. Produce—beef, corn, tobacco, and wheat. Madison County has the highest percentage (48) in the state of residents engaged in farming.

Madison County Seat—Marshall, North Carolina 28753   77

Martin County was established in 1774 from Halifax and Tyrrell Counties and named for Josiah Martin, the last royal governor of North Carolina.

The popularity of Governor Alexander Martin (1782–1785, 1789–1792) prevented the county name from changing. Williamston was named for William Williams, a prominent local citizen. The county seat was laid out in 1779 on land previously called Squhawky and owned by Thomas Hunter.

In 1775 the original wooden courthouse was built on stilts along the Roanoke River and was entered from boats. It burned in 1835 and was replaced by the present brick courthouse in 1887. This courthouse is on the *National Register of Historic Places* and is being restored. In 1985, a modern Metro County Governmental Center was constructed.

The Roanoke River forms the northern border of the county and runs through swamps and wetlands to the sea.

Census: 1950—27,938; 1995—25,848
Per capita income: $15,763
Land area: 481 square miles; elev. 60 ft.
Of Interest: Schools—Martin Community College in Williamston. Produce—tobacco, soybeans, corn, cotton, hogs, beef cattle, and chickens. Industry—paper, chemicals, apparel, textiles, wood, and food processing.

 # Mecklenberg County was

established in 1762 from Anson County and named for Queen Charlotte Sophia, Duchess of Mecklenberg and the wife of King George III of England. Her name was also given to the county seat.

The first courthouse was erected in 1762. A second courthouse, built in 1836, was replaced in 1897. The fourth courthouse, designed by architect Louis H. Asbury, was completed in 1928 and is on the *National Register of Historic Places*. The current, large, modern courthouse complex was completed in 1977; Wolf Associates of Charlotte were the architects.

Mecklenberg County is the most populous county in the state.

Census: 1950—197,052; 1995—577,773
Per capita income: $24,612
Land area: 542 square miles; elev. 795 ft.
Of Interest: Schools—(in Charlotte) Central Piedmont Community College, Johnson C. Smith University, Queens College, UNC-Charlotte, University Medical and Research Center, and (in Davidson) Davidson College. Tourist Attractions—birthplace of President Polk, Carowinds Theme Park, Lake Norman, Mint Museum, Coliseum, and Independence Arena. Industry—diversified industrial products and a major financial center.

 **Mitchell County** was established in 1861 and separated from Yancey County because of its Union sympathies at the time of the Civil War. The county was named for the Reverend Elisha Mitchell, a professor who fell to his death while exploring Mt. Mitchell, the highest peak east of the Mississippi River. The county seat was first in Calhoun, then moved to Davis (named for the Confederate president) in 1866. The name changed to Bakersville in 1868, and was named for pioneer David Baker.

A brick courthouse was built in 1868. The present courthouse was built in 1907, renovated in the 1960s, and is on the *National Register of Historic Places.*

Mitchell County is in the Toe River valley. The county is bordered by the Blue Ridge Parkway on the south and by Roan Mountain (5,960 ft.) and the Appalachian Trail on the north.

Census: 1950—15,143; 1995—14,738
Per capita income: $14,573
Land area: 220 square miles; elev. 2,550 ft.
Of Interest: Schools—Mayland Community College in Spruce Pine. Cultural Treasure—The Penland School of Crafts. Natural Heritage Site—Museum of North Carolina Minerals. Mines—mica, feldspar, and gemstones. Produce—dairy cattle, beef, tobacco, and corn. Industry—textiles, non-electrical machinery, furniture, wood, stone, and clay products.

Mitchell County Seat—Bakersville, North Carolina 28705   81

 **Montgomery County** was established in 1779 and named for Revolutionary hero General Richard Montgomery, who, in 1775 while attempting to conquer Canada, lost his life in the battle of Quebec. Troy is named for the ancient Greek city.

The first court was held in the home of Henry Munger near what is now Lawrenceville. In 1816 a courthouse was built in Lawrenceville. This courthouse burned in 1835, and a rented building was used until the new courthouse was completed in Troy in 1855. In 1886 this courthouse was demolished and a large wooden courthouse of "queer" design was erected. In 1904 a brick annex was added. In 1921 the present courthouse was built at a cost of approximately $150,000. In 1976 a two-story addition was built onto the courthouse. The Montgomery County Courthouse is on the *National Register of Historic Places.*

Montgomery County is a scenic county, covered in large part by the Uwharrie National Forest and bounded by the Yadkin and Pee Dee Rivers. Badin and Tillery Lakes offer recreational activities.

Census: 1950—17,260; 1995—23,890
Per capita income: $15,136
Land area: 488 square miles; elev. 664 ft.
Of Interest: National Historic Landmark—The Town Creek Indian Mound at Mt. Gilead, a reconstructed 16th century Indian ceremonial center. Produce—peaches, tobacco, chickens, wheat, cotton, corn, and dairy cattle. Industry—transport equipment, textiles, apparel, and woodworking.

Moore County was established in
1784 and named for Captain Alfred Moore, later associate justice of the U.S. Supreme Court. Carthage was named for the ancient North African city of Carthage, which was destroyed by the Romans.

The first courthouse was built in 1784. A second courthouse was erected in 1820, burned in 1889, and was rebuilt in 1890. A new courthouse was built in 1923. A modern addition was added in recent years. The courthouse is on the *National Register of Historic Places*.

Southern Pines is the home of the World Golf Hall of Fame. Nearby Pinehurst, a resort community, is noted for its fairs, including the Jazz Festival in January and the Antique Fair in May.

Census: 1950—33,129; 1995—66,852
Per capita income: $21,458
Land area: 672 square miles; elev. 575 ft.
Of Interest: Schools—Sandhills Community College in Pinehurst. National Historic Landmark—The Pinehurst Historic District. Recreation—golf, equestrian activities (polo to harness racing), tennis, water sports, archery, trap and skeet shooting, bicycling, croquet, and lawn bowling. Produce—tobacco, cotton, soybeans, corn, and hogs. Industry—tourism and retirement communities.

Moore County Seat—Carthage, North Carolina 28327   83

 **Nash County** was established in 1777. Both the county and the county seat were named for General Francis Nash, who was mortally wounded while fighting beside General Washington at the Battle of Germantown during the Revolution.

The first court was held in the home of Micajah Thomas. Court met in temporary quarters until 1784 when the courthouse was finished. In 1833 the courthouse was demolished and a new courthouse was completed. This courthouse served until 1921 when the present courthouse was built. The Nash County Courthouse is on the *National Register of Historic Places*.

Nashville is a major railway freight center.

Census: 1950—59,919; 1995—84,081
Per capita income: $18,074
Land area: 552 square miles; elev. 180 ft.
Of Interest: Schools—N.C. Wesleyan College and Nash Community College are both in Rocky Mount. Tourist Attractions—Stonewall Manor and the City Lake Park. Produce—tobacco, corn, cotton, soybeans, peanuts, hogs, beef cattle, and chickens. Industry—textiles, apparel, transport equipment, printing, fabricated metals, wood, and chemicals.

New Hanover County was

established in 1729 from Craven County and named for King George I's native kingdom of Hanover. Wilmington was named in honor of Spencer Compton, Earl of Wilmington.

The first courthouse, built in 1730 on the corner of Front and Market Streets, was bright yellow-painted brick, it partially burned in 1798. Other fires occurred in 1819 and 1840. A second courthouse was built in 1840 on Princess Street between Second and Third Streets. In 1892 a third courthouse was built on the site of the former city pound. Many piles had to be driven into the swampy land to support the building. An addition was built in 1914 and an annex in 1924. The 1892 courthouse is on the *National Register of Historic Places*.

Wilmington, on the Cape Fear River, is an active railway terminal and port.

Census: 1950—63,272; 1995—139,758
Per capita income: $18,931
Land area: 194 square miles; elev. 38 ft.
Of Interest: Schools—UNC-Wilmington and Cape Fear Community College in Wilmington. National Historic Landmarks—Fort Fisher (a Confederate strong point that was finally defeated by the Union Army and Navy) and the U.S.S. *North Carolina* of World War II fame, which offers hands-on self-guided tours. Cultural Treasures—Bellamy Mansion, the Museum of History and Design Arts, the Historic District, and Thalian Hall (a cultural center built in the 1800s). Industry—tourism and shipping.

New Hanover County Seat—Wilmington, North Carolina 28401 85

Northampton County was

established in 1741 and named for James Compton, Earl of Northampton. The county seat was named for Andrew Jackson, seventh president of the United States.

A wooden courthouse was built in 1741 in the village of Northampton Court House (renamed Jackson in 1826). In 1831 a separate fireproof office building was built on the square and stands today as the oldest building in the county; militia troops were quartered in this building during the Nat Turner slave insurrection in 1831. In 1858, the present courthouse was built in the style of a Greek temple. Major renovations were made in 1939 which added a large two-story block that gave the building a T-shape. Northampton County Courthouse is on the *National Register of Historic Places*.

At one time, there were many large plantations in the Roanoke River valley. Mowfield, Verona, and

Silver Mill plantations are open to visitors. The Sir Archie Restaurant (home of the Northampton Jockey Club) is noted for fine food. The area is famous for horse breeding and horse racing.

Census: 1950—28,432; 1955—20,665
Per capita income: $14,297
Land area: 540 square miles; elev. 131 ft.
Of Interest: Courthouse, Calvert House, Town Hall (now a bank), The Elms, Peebles House, St. Catherine's Hall, Northampton County Museum and Country Doctor's Office, and cotton gin. Recreation—Lake Gaston and Roanoke Rapids Lake. Produce—peanuts, cotton, soybeans, wheat, hogs, and chickens. Industry—apparel, wood, and administrative/research facilities.

 **Onslow County** was established in 1734 and named for Arthur Onslow, speaker of the House of Commons in the British Parliament for thirty years. In 1842 the county seat at Wantland Ferry was renamed Jacksonville in honor of Andrew Jackson.

The first courthouse was built on the New River in 1734. The second, built in Johnston in 1741, was destroyed by a storm in 1752. The third courthouse, completed in 1756 at Wantland Ferry, was replaced by the fourth in 1787. In 1885, a fifth was built at a cost of $24,000. When the building was condemned in 1947, the courthouse was drastically remodeled and enlarged; the architect was John J. Rowland of Kinston.

Census: 1950—35,077; 1995—147,840
Per capita income: $13,168
Land area: 756 square miles; elev. 23 ft.
Of Interest: Schools—Coastal Carolina Community College in Jacksonville. *National Register of Historic Places*— Onslow County Museum and Swansboro Village. Major Attractions—Hammocks Beach State Park and Topsoil Island, nesting places of endangered sea turtles. Also known for Camp Lejeune, fine beaches, marshes, migrating birds, alligators, fresh and saltwater fishing, and golf.

Onslow County Seat—Jacksonville, North Carolina 28540   87

Orange County was established
in 1752 and named for William of Orange who became King William III of England. Hillsborough is named for Lord Hillsborough.

In 1753 court was held in the home of James Watson. In 1755 a wooden courthouse was built. A brick courthouse, built in 1782, burned in 1789. A third courthouse, built of wood, was moved in 1845 to the intersection of Church and Queen Streets. In 1952 the present courthouse was built at a cost of $250,000 and is part of the Hillsborough Historic District. The old courthouse became part of Dickerson Chapel of the A.M.E. Church and is on the *National Register of Historic Places*.

Orange County, the home of the University of North Carolina at Chapel Hill, is part of the Research Triangle Park, which is comprised of educational and research facilities of UNC, North Carolina State University, and Duke University, and houses centers of research for Burroughs Wellcome, Northern Telecom, Glaxco, and IBM.

Census: 1950—34,435; 1995—105,844
Per capita income: $21,945
Land area: 398 square miles; elev. 543 ft.
Of Interest: Schools—UNC-Chapel Hill. National Historic Landmarks—Nash-Hooper House, Old East at UNC, and Playmaker's Theatre. Cultural Treasures—Ackland Art Museum, Arts Center, Hill Hall, Hillsborough Historic District, Memorial Hall, Morehead Planetarium, and North Carolina Botanical Garden. Attractions—Dean Smith Center (home of TarHeel basketball), Hillsborough Hog Day, Orange County Speedway, Apple Chill, and Festifall.

Pamlico County was established in 1822 and named for Pamlico Sound, which was named for an Indian tribe in eastern North Carolina. Bayboro was named for its proximity to the Bay River.

A rented building was used as the courthouse until the first courthouse was built in 1893 at a cost of $3,550. In 1938 the Works Progress Administration funded the building of the present brick courthouse in Bayboro.

Pamlico County is a peninsula surrounded by the Neuse River, the confluence of the Pamlico and Pungo Rivers and the Pamlico Sound.

> **Census:** 1950—9,993; 1995—11,856
> **Per capita income:** $14,905
> **Land area:** 341 square miles; elev. 13 ft.
> **Of Interest:** Schools—Pamlico Community College in Grantsboro. Produce—soybeans, corn, hogs, and chickens. Industry—seafood processing and apparel manufacturing.

Pasquotank County was established in 1670 and named for an Indian word meaning "where the stream forks." Elizabeth City was named in 1794 for Queen Elizabeth.

The first courthouse was located on the Pasquotank River, two miles from Elizabeth City. A second courthouse was built at Nixonton in 1770. A brick courthouse was built in Elizabeth City in 1800. As the Federal fleet was approaching in 1862, the sheriff burned the courthouse and his home next door. The courthouse was rebuilt in 1866. The present courthouse was completed in 1883 at a cost of $25,000 and is on the *National Register of Historic Places*. Court records, hidden by Arthur Jones in a barn during the Civil War, date back to 1700.

The Great Dismal Swamp occupies a large portion of the county. The Little River, Albemarle Sound, and the Pasquotank River form three borders of the county.

Census: 1950—24,347; 1995—33,304
Per capita income: $15,369
Land area: 229 square miles; elev. 12 ft.
Of Interest: Schools—College of The Albemarle in Elizabeth City and Elizabeth City State University. The Intracoastal Waterway is near Elizabeth City, a commercial fishing port. Produce—soybeans, corn, wheat, and hogs. Industry—transport equipment, apparel, textiles, furniture, and paper.

Pasquotank County Seat—Elizabeth City, North Carolina 27909   91

Pender County was established in 1875 and named for Confederate General William D. Pender, who was killed in the Battle of Gettysburg. The name of the county seat, originally Stanford, was changed in 1879 to Burgaw, and was named for an Indian group who lived along the Burgaw stream.

The first wooden courthouse also served as a store and a school. In 1885 a courthouse with a jail was built and was used until a new courthouse was dedicated on November 7, 1937. The Pender County Courthouse is on the *National Register of Historic Places.*

Large forests with game shelters occupy the low-lying eastern area of the county. Moore's Creek National Battlefield is in the west, near the Black River.

Census: 1950—18,423; 1995—34,710
Per capita income: $14,759
Land area: 857 square miles; elev. 49 ft.
Of Interest: Produce—soybeans, tobacco, peanuts, corn, hogs, chickens, and turkeys. The coastal area has commercial fishing.

Perquimans County was established in 1668 from a precinct of Albemarle County, Virginia, and named for an Indian tribe whose name, *Yeopim*, meant "land of beautiful women." Hertford was incorporated in 1758 and named for the Marquis of Hertford.

Courts first met in private homes. In 1722 the first courthouse was built of wood at Phelps Point on the Perquimans River, the future site of Hertford. In 1824 a second courthouse was built. Many renovations, including a major restoration in 1932 made possible by the generosity of Clinton White Toms, preserved the 1824 building. The Perquimans County Courthouse is on the *National Register of Historic Places*. A monument on the courthouse lawn honors a famous native son, baseball star Catfish Hunter, who was inducted into the Baseball Hall of Fame in 1987.

Albemarle Sound offers hunting, fishing, and sailing. The Newbold-White House, the oldest brick house in the state, was built in 1685. The Indian Summer Festival draws large crowds. Horseback riding is a favorite sport.

Census: 1950—9,620; 1995—10,663
Per capita income: $14,412
Land area: 261 square miles; elev. 15 ft.
Of Interest: Tourist Attractions—Albemarle Plantation and the Sound Links championship golf course. Produce—soybeans, corn, peanuts, cotton, and truck farming.

Person County was established in 1791 and named for General Thomas Person, a Revolutionary patriot, member of the Council of Safety, and a trustee of the University of North Carolina. He donated a large sum of money for the erection of Person Hall at the University of North Carolina. Roxboro, named for Roxburgh in Scotland, was established as the county seat in 1793.

Court was held first in Pope's Tavern. The first courthouse was built of logs in 1793. This courthouse was replaced by a frame building in 1810. A third courthouse, built of brick in 1873, was used until 1930 when the present courthouse was built. Charles C. Hartman was the architect and George W. Kane was the builder. An addition to the courthouse was built in 1975. The Person County Courthouse is on the *National Register of Historic Places.*

Person County, located in the north central piedmont, is largely agricultural. Hyco Lake is a popular recreational area.

Census: 1950—24,361; 1995—32,067
Per capita income: $16,849
Land area: 400 square miles; elev. 671 ft.
Of Interest: Recreation—water sports on Hyco Lake. Produce—tobacco, wheat, corn, soybeans, hogs, and dairy and beef cattle. Industry—technical instruments, textiles, transportation equipment, and primary metals.

Pitt County was established in 1760 from Beaufort County and named for William Pitt, Earl of Chatham. The county seat was first named Martinsboro and changed to honor Revolutionary hero General Nathanael Greene.

The first courthouse was erected in Log Town. A second courthouse, built in Greenville, burned in 1858 due to arson. The courthouse was promptly rebuilt and it, too, burned in 1910. The present courthouse, designed by the architectural firm of Milburn and Heister of Washington, D.C., is on the *National Register of Historic Places*. It is recorded that George Washington once visited Greenville in 1791.

Pitt county is in the Tar-Pamlico River valley.

Census: 1950—63,789; 1995—117,468
Per capita income: $17,679
Land area: 656 square miles; elev. 64 ft.
Of Interest: Schools—East Carolina University in Greenville and Pitt Community College in Greenville. Products—corn, tobacco, peanuts, soybeans, wheat, hogs, and chickens. Industry—transport equipment, chemicals, wood, textile, apparel, printing, and food processing.

 ***Polk County*** was established in 1854–1855 from Rutherford and Henderson Counties and named for Colonel William Polk, distinguished in the battles of Germantown, Brandywine, and Eutaw. Polk was wounded in all three battles. The county seat was named for the explorer Christopher Columbus.

The courthouse was completed in 1859 at a cost of $16,836, and is still in use. The Polk County Courthouse is on the *National Register of Historic Places*.

Polk County is located between mountains and the piedmont area of the state. Eastern hills are heavily wooded with Virginia pine, while the western mountains are forested with oak and hickory. The Green River flows into the Broad River at the eastern county line.

Census: 1950—11,627; 1995—15,714
Per capita income: $22,186
Land area: 234 square miles; elev. 1,145 ft.
Of Interest: Natural Heritage Site—Pearson's Falls. An early block house and fort were built at Point Lookout to protect the settlers from the Indians. A lead mine near the fort was used to make bullets and fish line sinkers. Legend has it that Step's Cove near Point Lookout always remains warm from the fire the Cherokee warriors built in 1799 to burn the son of Fannie Stepp. She was tied to a tree and forced to watch her son's death. Each spring, the Block House Steeplechase attracts large crowds. Produce—corn, soybeans, chickens, and dairy cows. Industry—fabricated metals and textiles.

Randolph County was established in 1779 from Guilford County and named for Peyton Randolph, president of the

Continental Congress. Asheboro was named for Governor Samuel Ashe, a North Carolina governor who served from 1792 to 1795.

The first courthouse was built in 1781 and replaced in 1835. The present courthouse was constructed in 1908; the architects were Wheeler, Runge, and Dickey of Charlotte and the builder was Joseph T. Owen.

The Uwharrie National Forest is located in Randolph County.

Census: 1950—50,804; 1995—115,543
Per capita income: $17,127
Land area: 801 square miles; elev. 879 ft.
Of Interest: Schools—Randolph Community College in Asheboro. Points of Interest—North Carolina Zoological Park, Covered Bridge, Seagrave Handicraft Pottery, American Classic Motorcycle Museum, Richard Petty Museum, Caraway Speedway, Back Creek, Dodton and Sandy Lakes, the Deep River, and many street festivals and fairs. Produce—tobacco, corn, wheat, soybeans, hogs, and beef cattle. Industry—rubber, plastic, leather goods, furniture, textiles, and precision instruments.

Randolph County Seat—Asheboro, North Carolina 27203   97

Richmond County was established in 1779 and named for Charles Lennox, Duke of Richmond, who sought independence for the American colonies in the British House of Lords. Rockingham was named for Charles Watson of Wentworth, the Marquis of Rockingham.

The first courthouse was built in 1780 and replaced in 1884. In 1923 the current courthouse was completed at a cost of $20,000. This courthouse is on the *National Register of Historic Places*.

Forest covers much of the county. The Sandhills Recreation Area, Sandhills Gameland, Pee Dee National Wildlife Refuge, Blewett Falls Lake, and Lake Tillery comprise some 3,000 acres of recreational water. Large crowds are drawn to the NASCAR stock car races held at the Rockingham Speedway Complex for sport cars, trucks, carts, and motorcycles.

Census: 1950—39,597; 1995—45,452
Per capita income: $14,454
Land area: 477 square miles; elev. 211 ft.
Of Interest: Schools—Richmond Community College in Hamlet. Produce—chickens and turkeys. Manufacturing—paper products, textiles, plastics, pharmaceuticals, furniture, sailboats, and metal machinery.

Robeson County was established in 1787 and named for Colonel Thomas Robeson of the Revolutionary Army. Lumberton was named for the Lumber River.

The first temporary courthouse was built in Lumberton in 1787 and replaced by a substantial wooden courthouse in 1788. In 1848 a court-house was built for $7,500. This courthouse was replaced in 1908 at a cost of $75,000; Frank P. Milburn was the architect. In 1974 the current modern courthouse replaced the 1908 building.

Robeson County is home to the Lumbee Indians, the largest tribe east of the Mississippi, who are said to be descendants of the "Lost Colony." Their history is commem-orated in Pembroke's Native American Resource Center, the Indian Cultural Center, and a popular outdoor drama entitled *Strike at the Wind.*

Census: 1950—87,769; 1995—110,825
Per capita income: $14,024
Land area: 944 square miles; elev. 137 ft.
Of Interest: Schools—UNC-Pembroke in Pembroke and the Robeson Community College in Lumberton. Points of Interest—Flora MacDonald Gardens in Red Springs (site of old Flora MacDonald College), Springtime Dogwood Trail, Highland Games, re-enactment of a Revolutionary War Battle, downtown historic Lumberton (on the *National Register of Historic Places*), and Fairmont's Border Belt Farmers Museum. Produce—corn, soybeans, tobacco, cotton, wheat, peanuts, potatoes, hogs, and turkeys. Industry—transport equipment, preci-sion instruments, food processing, textiles, wood, electrical equipment, printing, furniture, and chemicals.

Robeson County Seat—Lumberton, North Carolina 28358   99

Rockingham County was

established in 1785. Both county and county seat were named for Charles Watson of Wentworth, Marquis of Rockingham, a leader of the British Parliament who advocated independence for the American colonies.

The first courthouse was built of wood at Eagle Falls, later named Jackson. In 1824 the second courthouse was built in Wentworth. This building was demolished and a new courthouse was erected in 1850, renovated in 1882, and destroyed by fire in 1906. The fourth present courthouse was built in 1908 for around $25,000; the architect was Frank P. Milburn of Washington, D.C. The building was renovated and enlarged in 1972. A large county government complex was built in 1980. However, the 1908 courthouse continues in service as the register of deeds.

Rockingham County is in the Haw River valley. More than half the county is forested. Belews Lake on the Dan River offers recreation. An Amish community is located in Hamptonville.

> **Census:** 1950—64,815; 1995—88,512
> **Per capita income:** $16,979
> **Land area:** 572 square miles; elev. 900 ft.
> **Of Interest:** Schools—Rockingham Community College in Wentworth. Tourist Attractions—The Chinqua-Penn Plantation House at Reidsville has furnishings, Byzantine mosaics, and altar pieces from the fifteenth century. Produce—tobacco, corn, wheat, soybeans, and dairy cattle. Industry—textiles, apparel, printing, and rubber, plastic, and leather goods.

Rowan County was established in

1752 and named for Matthew Rowan, acting colonial governor at the time. The county seat was called Rowan Court House until 1755 when it was named Salisbury for the Marquis of Salisbury.

A major railway center and steam railway repair facility of the southern system was located at Spencer, halfway between Washington, D.C., and Atlanta, and is now preserved as the North Carolina Transportation Museum. Famous historical figures associated with Rowan County are Squire Boone, father of Daniel Boone, and Andrew Jackson, who studied law in Salisbury.

Census: 1950—75,410; 1995—118,963
Per capita income: $16,841
Land area: 517 square miles; elev. 764 ft.
Of Interest: Schools—Catawba College, Livingstone College, and Rowan-Cabarrus Community College. Historic Sites—Josephus Hall House, Old Stone House, Lazy 5 Ranch (exotic animals), Waterworks Visual Arts Center, Rowan Museum, W. J. Walls Heritage Hall (with many African artifacts), and the Sloan Park/Kerr Mill. Produce—soybeans, corn, wheat, cotton, dairy products, beef cattle, and chickens. Industry—primary metals, chemicals, transport equipment, textiles, apparel, printing, food processing, and metal, glass, stone, clay, rubber, plastic, and leather products.

Rutherford County was established in 1779. Both the county and the county seat were named for Griffith Rutherford, a prominent Revolutionary patriot. Rutherfordton was established in 1787.

Court was held in private homes until 1802 when a log courthouse was built at Shepherd's Landing (now called Holland's Creek). The second courthouse, built of brick at Rutherfordton in 1834, burned on Christmas Day 1907. A replacement was built in 1908. The present stately courthouse was completed in 1926; funded by $250,000 in bonds. The architect was Louis H. Asbury.

The county lies in the Broad River valley, and is forested with pine in the west and hardwoods in the northwest. The main recreational area is around Lake Lure.

Census: 1950—46,356; 1995—59,022
Per capita income: $15,791
Land area: 568 square miles; elev. 1,096 ft.
Of Interest: Natural Heritage Sites—Chimney Rock Park and Hickory Nut Gorge (including Bat Cave). Cultural Treasure—St. John's Episcopal Church. Produce—tobacco, cotton, corn, wheat, soybeans, peanuts, and peaches. Industry—textiles, paper, furniture, apparel, and rubber/plastic/leather fabrication.

Sampson County was established in 1784 and named for Colonel John Sampson, a member of the House of Commons in England. Clinton was established in 1818 and named for DeWitt Clinton, governor of New York.

The first courthouse was built of wood in 1785. In 1853 a new building was erected on the same site. The present courthouse was built in 1904. Between 1937 and 1939, extensive renovations, partly funded by the Works Progress Administration, were made. A new jail was built at a cost of $40,500.

Sampson County is the largest in size of North Carolina's one hundred counties. The Laurel Lake Gardens, where camellias have their peak bloom from November to April, are a major attraction.

Census: 1950—49,780; 1995—50,576
Per capita income: $19,123
Land area: 963 square miles; elev. 158 ft.
Of Interest: Schools—Sampson Community College in Clinton. Produce—corn, cotton, tobacco, soybeans, wheat, peanuts, cattle, hogs, turkeys, and chickens. Industry—food processing, woodwork, electrical equipment, textiles, apparel, and machinery.

Sampson County Seat—Clinton, North Carolina 28328 105

Scotland County was established
in 1899 from Richmond County and named for the many Scots who were early settlers. Laurinburg was named for the prominent McLaurin family.

The first courthouse was built in Laurinburg in 1901. In 1964 a new courthouse was erected and designed by W. E. Matthews of Laurinburg.

The Sandhills Game Land occupies much of the northern part of the county, which is also the home of Camp MacKall Military Reservation.

Census: 1950—33,763; 1995—34,766
Per capita income: $15,352
Land area: 317 square miles; elev. 227 ft.
Of Interest: Schools—St. Andrews Presbyterian College in Laurinburg. Produce—cotton, soybeans, corn, tobacco, peanuts, wheat, beef cattle, and hogs. Industry—precision instruments, primary metals, plastic, leather goods, electrical equipment, textiles, furniture, and chemicals.

Stanly County was established in

1841 from Montgomery County and named for John Stanly, speaker of the House of Commons. Tradition has it that Stanly County was formed after a fire, set by a defendant seeking to destroy incriminating evidence, completely destroyed the Montgomery County Courthouse. After some controversy, it was decided to split Montgomery County and form Stanly County. Albemarle was named for the Duke of Albemarle, one of the Lords Proprietors.

The first courthouse was built in 1842 in Albemarle and replaced in 1893. The courthouse was remodeled in 1926–1927 and, although it suffered from a fire in 1928, continued in service until 1972. The present four-story courthouse was designed by Williams and Associates.

The eastern border of Stanly County is formed by the Yadkin-Pee Dee River system including Badin and Tillery Lakes. The Rocky River is on the southern border. The Morrow Mountain State Park, part of the Uwharrie Mountain Range, is popular for recreation, swimming, boating, fishing, and skiing.

Census: 1950—37,130; 1995—53,865
Per capita income: $16,152
Land area: 399 square miles; elev. 505 ft.
Of Interest: Schools—Stanly Community College in Albemarle and Pfeiffer College in Misenheimer. National Historic Landmark—The Hardaway Site. Produce—soybeans, wheat, corn, milk cows, and egg production. Industry—textiles, apparel, electrical equipment, and metals.

Stanly County Seat—Albemarle, North Carolina 28001   107

 **Stokes County** was established in 1789 and named for Colonel John Stokes, a Revolutionary War hero and a district judge. Danbury was named in 1853 for the Dan River.

The first courthouse was built in 1790 at Germantown. The next courthouse was built in 1833. The county seat was moved to Crawford (later Danbury) in 1849 and a court-house was completed in 1851. The name was changed to Danbury in 1853. This courthouse was replaced in 1904 by one designed by Wheeler of Charlotte. A large Stokes County Government Center, located on the edge of this small community (no traffic light) is enhanced by a generous parking area and jail, and now serves as the courthouse. The handsome 1904 building is used by the Board of Education.

The Dan River flows through the county and is dammed to form Belews Lake. Hanging Rock State Park is a natural wonder.

Census: 1950—21,520; 1995—41,102
Per capita income: $16,399
Land area: 459 square miles; elev. 825 ft.
Of Interest: Schools—Mount Olive College in Mount Olive. Produce—corn, tobacco, wheat, soybeans, apples, chickens, hogs, and beef. Industry—transport equipment and tobacco processing.

 **Surry County** was established in 1770 and named for Lord Surry, an English nobleman who opposed taxation for the colonies. Dobson was named for Colonel Dobson of the Revolutionary Army.

Court was first held in the home of Gidion Wright. The county seat moved from place to place and courthouses were built in each location: Richmond in 1774, Rockford in 1792, and finally, Dobson in 1855. The courthouse in Dobson deteriorated over time, and in 1916, after much urging by Superior Court Judge E. B. Cline, the present courthouse was built. Wings were added in 1971.

The Yadkin River borders the county on the south.

Census: 1950—45,593; 1995—65,260
Per capita income: $17,406
Land area: 537 square miles; elev. 1,265 ft.
Of Interest: Schools—Surry Community College in Dobson. State Heritage Site—Pilot Mountain State Park. Pilot Mountain, a quartzitic monadnock, rises 1,500 ft. above the surrounding land and dominates the county. (Forms a tube of rock into a tower. This tower guides pilots in the area.) State Living Historical Site—Hope Creek Farm, near Pinnacle. Cultural Treasure—Mount Airy Museum of Regional History. Produce—corn, wheat, tobacco, soybeans, dairy and beef cattle, and chickens. Industry—electrical equipment, textiles, apparel, stone, clay, glass, rubber, plastic, and leather products.

 **Swain County** was established in 1871 and named for David L. Swain, governor of North Carolina and president of the University of North Carolina. Bryson City was named in honor of Colonel Thaddeus Dillard Bryson.

The first courthouse, built in 1872, burned, and was rebuilt in 1880. In 1908 a classic courthouse was built for $35,000. This building is now a senior citizens' hall. The present one-story brick courthouse was built in 1980.

Swain County is nestled in the Great Smoky Mountains National Park.

Census: 1950—9,921; 1995—11,574
Per capita income: $12,108
Land area: 530 square miles; elev. 1,737 ft.
Of Interest: Cultural Treasures—*Unto These Hills* theatrical production, Oconaluftee Indian Village, and the Cherokee Qualla Arts and Craft Museum. Attractions—scenic railway and Nantahala Gorge. Produce—corn and tobacco.

Swain County Seat—Bryson City, North Carolina 28713   *111*

Transylvania County was

established in 1861. The name means "across the woods" in Latin. Brevard was named in honor of Colonel Ephriam Brevard, a Revolutionary War hero.

The first court was held in the home of B. C. Lankford, near Straus School. A brick courthouse was completed in Brevard in 1881 at a cost of $12,000. This courthouse was expanded and a jail added in 1921. In 1983 the three-story brick tower was renovated, keeping the same outside appearance. The tower clock was donated by local citizens in 1984. The courthouse is on the *National Register of Historic Places*.

The headwaters of the French Broad River are in the Blue Ridge Mountains of Transylvania County. The Pisgah and Nantahala National Forests cover the western part of the

county. Ways to protect the forests are demonstrated at the Cradle of Forestry in America near Brevard.

Census: 1950—15,194; 1995—27,226
Per capita income: $17,131
Land area: 379 square miles; elev. 2,230 ft.
Of Interest: Schools—Brevard College. Natural Heritage Sites—Pink Beds, Looking Glass Rock, Devil's Courthouse, and Whitewater Falls. Sliding Rock provides an exciting wet slide to the young in heart and body. Cultural Treasure—Brevard Music Center. Produce—corn and tobacco. Mining—Asbestos is mined commercially. Industry—precision instruments, paper, non-electrical machinery, textiles, and chemicals.

Tyrrell County was established in 1729 and named for Lord Proprietor Sir John Tyrrell of Essex, who served under George II of England. The county seat, originally named Elizabeth Town, became Columbia in 1810 in honor of Christopher Columbus.

Court was held in private homes until 1749 when the first courthouse was built on Kendrick's Creek near what is now Roper. In 1801 a courthouse was built in Elizabeth Town (now Columbia). The present courthouse, built in 1903 in Columbia, is located on the Scuppernong River near the outlet to Bull Bay on Albemarle Sound.

Albemarle Sound borders the county on the north. The Intracoastal Waterway enters Albemarle Sound via the Alligator River on the eastern border. The eastern part of the county is swampy and is part of the Pocosin Lakes National Wildlife Refuge. Hardwood is found in the eastern and much of the southern part of the county as well as in the wetlands.

Census: 1950—5,048; 1995—3,786
Per capita income: $14,398
Land area: 399 square miles; elev. 10 ft.
Of Interest: Produce—potatoes, soybeans, corn, cotton, and hogs. Industry—logging and commercial fishing.

Tyrrell County Seat—Columbia, North Carolina 27925

Union County was established in 1842 and named for the American Union. Monroe was named for President James Monroe, fifth president of the United States.

The first courthouse was built in 1842. A second courthouse was built in 1886. From the steps of this courthouse on December 9, 1921, French Marshal Ferdinand Foch, Commander-in-Chief of the Allied Armies during World War I, decorated the colors of the 5th and 17th Field Artillery Regiments from Fort Bliss with the *Fourragere* of the French croix de guerre for conspicuous bravery with the American expeditionary forces in France.

A new modern courthouse was erected in 1972; architects were Henningson, Durham, and Richardson, Inc.

Cane Creek Park has recreational facilities for boating and swimming.

Census: 1950—42,034; 1995—98,134
Per capita income: $17,879
Land area: 643 square miles; elev. 576 ft.
Of Interest: Historic Waxhaw (home to the annual Highland Scottish Games), Andrew Jackson Museum, Charlotte Regional Steeplechase, and the Blooming Arts Festival each spring. Produce—livestock, poultry, turkeys, chickens, soybeans, wheat, cotton, corn, dairy products, and eggs. Industry—wood, fabricated metals, food processing, machinery, apparel, stone/clay/glass products, textiles, transport equipment, and furniture.

Vance County was established in
1881 and named for Zebulon Baird Vance,
U.S. congressman, North Carolina governor,
and U.S. senator. Henderson was named in honor of Chief Justice
Leonard Henderson.

Court was held in rented buildings from 1881–1884 until the first courthouse was completed at a cost of approximately $8,000. The courthouse was remodeled in 1908 by Milburn and Heister of Washington, D.C.

The Vance County Office Building was constructed in 1960 for non-judicial functions.

John H. Kerr Reservoir covers 12,800 acres and contains Kerr Lake State Recreation Area.

Census: 1950—32,101; 1995—40,104
Per capita income: $15,726
Land area: 269 square miles; elev. 513 ft.
Of Interest: Schools—Vance-Granville Community College in Henderson. Produce—tobacco, wheat, soybeans, and hogs. Industry—stone, glass, textiles, apparel, and tobacco products.

Wake County was established in 1770 and named for the Wake sisters, wife and sister-in-law of Colonial Governor William Tryon. The county seat of Raleigh was named for Sir Walter Raleigh and is also the capital of North Carolina.

The first courthouse was built of logs on Joel Lane's estate in 1771. The state capital, along with the county seat, was established in Raleigh in 1792. In 1795 a "large and elegant" courthouse was built on Fayetteville Street. This building was moved in 1835 to the corner of Wilmington and Davie Streets. In 1882 a brick courthouse was then constructed on the old site. Additions to this courthouse were made to the front of the building. A new courthouse was constructed in 1915 at cost of $275,000. The present twelve-story courthouse was built in 1970.

Wake County, a largely urban county, lies in the Neuse River valley where the Piedmont hills meet the Coastal Plain. Governmental services and education are primary activities.

Census: 1950—136,450; 1995—518,446
Per capita income: $23,959
Land area: 866 square miles; elev. 363 ft.
Of Interest: Schools—(Raleigh) N.C. State University, Peace College, St. Augustine's College, Shaw University, Meredith College, and Wake Community College. National Historic Landmarks—Christ Episcopal Church, Josephus Daniels House (Wakestone, Masonic Temple of Raleigh), and the State Capitol. Produce—milk, eggs, tobacco, soybeans, corn, and hogs. Industry—government, education, food processing, printing, fabricated metal, electrical equipment, and non-electrical machinery.

 **Warren County** was established in 1779. The county and the county seat were named for General Joseph Warren, a physician from Massachusetts, who fell while fighting at Bunker Hill.

The first courthouse was completed in 1783. In 1850 a second courthouse was built. This courthouse was replaced in 1906 by the present brick courthouse.

Warren County, situated in the Roanoke River valley, is noted historically for its large plantations. Warrenton Historic District is on the *National Register of Historic Places*. Recreation areas include part of Gaston Lake and part of the John H.

Kerr Reservoir with Kimball Point State Recreation Area and County Line State Recreation Area.

Census: 1950—23,539; 1995—18,096
Per capita income: $11,989
Land area: 445 square miles; elev. 451 ft.
Of Interest: Produce—tobacco, soybeans, peanuts, corn, wheat, cotton, and cattle. Industry—wood and food processing, textiles, and apparel.

Washington County was established in 1799 and named for George Washington, the first president of the United States of America. Plymouth was established as the county seat in 1823 and named for the first settlement in New England.

The first courthouse was built at Lee's Mill (now Roper) in 1799. A wooden courthouse was erected in Plymouth in 1823. This courthouse burned when bombarded by Federal troops during the Civil War. A third courthouse was built three years later and was burned by a carpetbagger who wished to destroy incriminating evidence. A custom house in Plymouth was then used as a courthouse, but in 1881 this structure also burned. A new courthouse was built in 1882. In 1918 the courthouse was demolished. The present courthouse was completed in 1919.

Plymouth is a major rail/freight terminal. In the north, there is commercial and sport fishing on Albemarle Sound near the mouth of the Roanoke River. In the southeast, Lake Phelps and Pettigrew State Park provide over 17,000 acres for boating, fishing, hiking, and recreation.

Census: 1950—13,180; 1995—13,744
Per capita income: $16,055
Land area: 337 square miles; elev. 21 ft.
Of Interest: Somerset antebellum plantation, the River Fest in June, the Civil War Living History Weekend in April, and Indian Heritage Week in September. Produce—corn, soybeans, sweet potatoes, peanuts, wheat, tobacco, hogs, and cattle. Industry— paper and wood products and apparel.

Watauga County was established in 1849 and given an Indian name meaning "whispering waters." Boone was named in honor of Daniel Boone, the pioneer hero.

The first courts were held in a barn on Joseph Hardin's farm, one mile east of Boone. The first courthouse was built of brick in 1850 and destroyed by fire in 1873. The second courthouse was built in 1874 and used until 1904 when it was converted into a bank and store. The 1904 courthouse was designed by architects Wheeler and Runger of Charlotte who designed similar courthouses in seven other counties. Until 1939 the courthouse was still heated by open fireplaces. This courthouse served until a new building was erected in 1968.

The Blue Ridge Parkway passes through the southeastern section of the county. Pisgah National Forest and Beech Mountain border the area. The Yadkin and Watauga Rivers flow through the county.

Census: 1950—18,342; 1995—40,195
Per capita income: $15,090
Land area: 320 square miles; elev. 3,266 ft.
Of Interest: Schools—Appalachian State University in Boone. Natural Heritage Sites—Grandfather Mountain (partly in the county), the Julian Price Memorial Park, Moses H. Cone Memorial Park, and The Southern Appalachian Historical Association's drama, *Horn in the West*, performed annually at Hickory Ridge Home. Tourist Attractions—Tweetsie Railroad, Mystery Hill, Valle Crucis, the Mast General Store, and Moses Cone National Park, Blowing Rock.

Wayne County was established in
1779 and named for General "Mad Anthony" Wayne, Revolutionary War hero. Goldsboro was named for an official of the Wilmington and Weldon Railroad.

The original county seat was in Waynesboro on the Neuse River, where in 1782, a wooden courthouse was built. In 1840 the second courthouse was built in the newly established Goldsboro. A third courthouse was built in 1913 at a cost of $110,000. An addition was built in 1954, and renovation took place in 1985 at a cost of $135,000. A county office building and jail have been built behind the courthouse.

Wayne County is on the coastal plane. Seymour Johnson Air Base is located near Goldsboro.

Census: 1950—64,267; 1995—111,056
Per capita income: $15,261
Land area: 555 square miles; elev. 111 ft.
Of Interest: Schools—Wayne Community College in Goldsboro. Historic Site—the log cabin birthplace of Charles B. Aycock, who as governor (1900–1904) inspired the growth of the public school system. Aycock's famous statement, "Equal! That is the word! On that word I plant myself and my party—the equal right of every child born on earth to have the opportunity to burgeon out all that is within him." Aycock died while making a speech on public education. Produce—chickens, turkeys, livestock, tobacco, soybeans, and corn.

Wilkes County was established in

1777. The county and the county seat were named for John Wilkes, the English politician who supported American rights at the time of the Revolution.

The original name of the county seat was Mulberry Field, where a log courthouse was built. In 1830 this building was moved and became a stable. A second courthouse was built, and in 1903 was replaced by the current courthouse. This courthouse was designed by the architects Wheeler and Runge of Charlotte, using a design they had used in Statesville and a number of other courthouses. The cost was $47,000. The Wilkes County Courthouse is on the *National Register of Historic Places*. The famous murder trial of Tom Dula (pronounced Dooley in the hill country), and his hanging on May 1, 1868, inspired the famous "Ballad of Tom Dooley." Dula was actually hung in Iredell County because of the passions in Wilkes County. However, an ancient

oak tree, dating from the 1800s, still stands just northeast of the Wilkes courthouse where Tories were hanged.

Wilkes County is in the foothills of the Blue Ridge Mountains, drained by the Yadkin River, and is heavily forested with pine and hardwoods.

Census: 1950—45,243; 1995—61,920
Per capita income: $16,657
Land area: 765 square miles; elev. 1,042 ft.
Of Interest: Schools—Wilkes Community College in Wilkesboro. Cultural Treasure—Old Wilkes Jail. Natural Heritage Site—Doughton Park. Produce—tobacco, corn, beef cattle, chickens, and eggs. Industry—food processing, furniture, apparel, transport equipment, stone, clay, glass, and wood products.

Wilson County was established in

1855. The county and the county seat were named for Louis D. Wilson, a member of the Constitutional Convention of 1835 and legislator from Buncombe County, who died of yellow fever as an officer in the Mexican War.

The first courthouse was built in 1855 and remodeled in 1902. It was razed in 1924 when the present courthouse was built. The Wilson County Courthouse has recently been remodeled and is on the *National Register of Historic Places*.

Wilson County is noted for a number of famous restaurants serving pit-cooked pork barbecue.

Census: 1950—45,243; 1995—68,042
Per capita income: $18,596
Land area: 373 square miles; elev. 147 ft.
Of Interest: Schools—Barton College and Wilson Technical Community College. Attractions—Imagination Station Science Museum, Southern National Speedway for stock car racing, and Tobacco Farm Life Museum in Kenly. Produce—tobacco, corn, soybeans, wheat, hogs, and chickens. Industry—tobacco processing, paper, apparel, food processing, and products of stone, clay, glass, rubber, plastics, and leather.

 *Yadkin County* was established in 1850. Both the county and the county seat were given the name Yadkin, an Indian word possibly meaning "big tree."

The first temporary courthouse was built in 1851 at Doweltown. The first courthouse at Yadkinville was built in 1855. Bricks were hand-made by slaves on the farm of Moti Holcomb. This courthouse was demolished in 1957, and a new courthouse was completed in 1959 at a cost of $400,000. The present courthouse was built in 1965.

The Yadkin River forms the northern and eastern boundaries of the county. Daniel Boone's father, Squire Boone, moved to Yadkin County in 1750 and was buried there in 1820.

Census: 1950—22,133; 1994—32,871
Per capita income: $16,761
Land area: 355 square miles; elev. 960 ft.
Of Interest: Produce—corn, tobacco, soybeans, wheat, beef cattle, and chickens. Industry—textiles and apparel.

Yancey County was established in

1833 and named for Bartlett Yancey, congressman and speaker of the state senate. Burnsville was named for Captain Otway Burns, hero of the War of 1812.

The first court was held in 1834 in the Cane River Church until a temporary structure was built. A permanent brick courthouse was built in 1836. In 1907 the building was demolished to form a grass square. A courthouse was built in 1908 and was replaced by the current courthouse in 1965. Yancey County Courthouse is on the *National Register of Historic Places.*

Nestled in the Pisgah National Forest, much of the county is covered by hickory, oak, and hemlock. The summit of Mount Mitchell, (6,684 ft., the highest mountain in the eastern United States) is in the county. The South Toe and Cane Rivers provide popular fishing and canoeing. The Blue Ridge Parkway follows the southern border of the county.

Census: 1950—12,433; 1995—16,111
Per capita income: $13,566
Land area: 311 square miles; elev. 2,817 ft.
Of Interest: Produce—apples, tobacco, corn, and beef and dairy cattle. Mining—asbestos, olivine, and mica. Industry—textiles and wood products.

Yancey County Seat—Burnsville, North Carolina 28714   *129*

County	Population per square mile	Non-agricultural wage/salary employees	Manufacturing employees	Unemployment rate (percentage)	Registered voters
Alamance	266.20	55,980	20,760	3.8	64,335
Alexander	116.53	9,840	5,860	3.6	19,582
Alleghany	41.65	3,430	1,350	6.8	6,855
Anson	44.74	8,740	4,070	10.1	12,167
Ashe	53.85	7,780	3,070	10.1	14,791
Avery	61.38	5,820	770	6.7	9,970
Beaufort	52.28	17,420	6,440	8.9	21,346
Bertie	29.80	6,680	3,610	7.4	11,324
Bladen	33.91	9,210	3,740	7.7	15,644
Brunswick	69.58	16,860	2,390	9.7	35,708
Buncombe	292.43	94,350	20,090	3.8	107,439
Burke	160.81	37,410	18,190	4.9	42,314
Cabarrus	306.68	42,420	14,890	3.6	64,814
Caldwell	154.84	32,630	17,680	3.9	37,555
Camden	26.44	1,140	60	4.7	4,010
Carteret	108.49	17,800	1,650	6.1	31,736
Caswell	48.85	3,100	780	3.8	11,486
Catawba	310.72	88,010	40,950	4.4	72,671
Chatham	60.64	13,290	6,290	2.8	25,831
Cherokee	48.16	7,450	2,610	7.0	15,953
Chowan	78.13	5,200	1,540	6.7	7,056
Clay	36.35	1,330	260	5.6	5,920
Cleveland	191.88	37,340	14,670	5.6	43,901
Columbus	54.52	18,730	5,910	7.0	30,388
Craven	118.62	32,110	4,040	5.6	40,295
Cumberland	445.05	95,060	12,170	5.6	108,711
Currituck	91.37	2,540	50	3.7	8,673
Dare	66.22	12,620	250	6.4	15,322
Davidson	248.93	47,550	22,590	3.3	71,715
Davie	112.82	9,690	4,301	3.7	16,622
Duplin	52.06	14,990	6,180	6.1	20,809
Durham	645.39	135,570	32,640	3.0	120,867
Edgecombe	110.90	23,070	6,770	8.8	33,423
Forsyth	661.15	158,170	33,810	3.4	158,905
Franklin	84.19	19,755	1,940	4.4	18,737
Gaston	505.60	81,300	35,980	4.2	86,634
Gates	27.89	1,390	230	3.4	5,444
Graham	25.88	2,180	700	17.3	5,552
Granville	75.67	15,950	6,000	4.7	18,854
Greene	62.30	3,070	640	4.7	7,800
Guilford	571.92	239,280	57,110	3.4	225,658
Halifax	79.20	20,360	5,540	9.6	26,501
Harnett	122.74	19,260	5,220	4.0	31,580
Haywood	92.01	15,570	3,990	6.0	32,604
Henderson	199.63	27,200	6,630	3.3	50,027
Hertford	63.04	8,410	1,920	6.0	12,707
Hoke	65.96	7,080	3,740	7.1	10,810
Hyde	8.22	1,640	310	11.1	3,191
Iredell	175.24	45,030	17,750	3.5	56,567
Jackson	58.13	10,750	1,340	6.0	17,453

Democrats	Republicans	Active physicians	Hospital beds	Prison admissions; Parole population	Traffic accidents; Fatalities	Live births	Deaths
36,317	21,363	62	188	539; 513	2,949; 16	1,438	1,147
8,782	9,047	7	44	67; 47	607; 5	384	248
4,679	1,824	6	46	15; 9	287; 2	84	135
10,437	1,312	9	30	86; 83	606; 8	360	239
7,194	6,664	12	55	30; 24	481; 3	235	290
1,627	7,312	13	83	11; 19	361; 1	211	171
15,155	5,101	21	148	129; 168	1,319; 12	519	486
10,270	814	8	16	86; 76	382; 5	285	249
13,040	1,919	11	52	129; 129	709; 13	428	325
19,648	12,777	19	88	122; 160	1,256; 22	750	576
60,560	36,192	180	656	384; 421	5,608; 23	2,238	2,019
22,145	15,925	55	206	199; 143	2,290; 17	1,082	768
31,011	26,534	62	331	336; 258	2,905; 13	1,438	861
16,733	16,852	40	100	233; 227	1,325; 10	956	664
3,103	558	0	0	9; 7	101; 1	78	62
16,073	11,941	30	117	96; 99	1,244; 6	646	535
9,512	1,502	7	0	48; 67	603; 7	244	233
29,039	33,858	87	330	410; 358	4,401; 21	1,692	1,132
16,716	6,702	18	35	80; 85	1,175; 15	560	397
8,014	6,461	17	102	27; 22	404; 1	238	242
5,261	1,348	12	50	21; 26	244; 3	190	192
2,671	2,432	2	0	2; 5	143; 1	66	77
29,140	11,218	46	288	209; 250	2,400; 23	1,268	914
24,751	4,575	22	136	170; 124	1,308; 29	757	559
22,976	12,921	50	232	184; 216	1,658; 14	1,504	699
66,995	27,983	148	433	500; 701	7,480; 49	5,599	1,743
5,424	2,014	3	0	31; 17	394; 9	187	170
8,479	4,811	12	0	48; 30	590; 3	266	180
33,118	33,345	57	183	346; 364	2,985; 37	1,764	1,194
5,758	9,660	12	46	65; 52	572; 7	332	269
15,848	4,447	18	40	143; 107	1,348; 18	659	521
78,197	26,972	513	1,071	390; 436	6,625; 25	2,970	1,614
27,700	4,395	19	100	235; 302	1,383; 12	921	642
82,579	58,822	342	1,413	573; 781	7,459; 28	3,836	2,498
13,267	4,497	12	52	139; 94	734; 12	540	410
45,312	33,974	88	343	347; 404	4,848; 27	2,506	1,732
4,626	541	2	0	12; 13	196; 3	126	109
2,607	2,543	3	0	8; 10	144; 1	96	85
15,013	2,853	24	66	133; 139	993; 6	543	426
6,603	915	3	0	37; 40	457; 3	184	137
122,914	77,818	266	1,017	878; 1,003	13,971; 63	5,053	3,201
22,084	3,227	25	158	257; 202	1,331; 29	834	678
20,960	8,670	23	105	179; 238	1,919; 20	1,256	694
21,033	8,542	31	130	81; 81	932; 16	535	514
17,495	25,479	57	213	179; 130	1,733; 16	810	925
11,172	1,318	17	104	117; 89	497; 9	318	252
8,451	1,536	6	0	133; 517	514; 11	499	192
2,855	220	1	0	7; 8	106; 2	53	76
28,983	22,379	55	395	457; 308	2,453; 19	1,402	985
10,307	5,315	29	86	32; 35	590; 4	308	253

County	Population per square mile	Non-agricultural wage/salary employees	Manufacturing employees	Unemployment rate (percentage)	Registered voters
Johnston	120.14	26,780	7,510	3.0	46,221
Jones	20.40	1,530	220	5.7	5,629
Lee	204.44	24,320	11,000	4.7	21,440
Lenoir	151.39	30,290	8,790	6.7	27,980
Lincoln	170.76	16,210	7,080	4.8	31,757
McDowell	84.29	16,590	9,350	6.2	19,999
Macon	50.68	8,110	1,370	4.1	—
Madison	38.97	3,290	910	4.3	12,705
Martin	53.74	11,050	5,300	6.7	13,417
Mecklenburg	1,064.09	387,350	49,270	3.1	326.038
Mitchell	66.99	5,390	1,920	8.6	9,872
Montgomery	48.95	10,640	5,690	7.1	13,182
Moore	99.48	29,510	5,760	3.9	38,082
Nash	152.32	41,230	13,770	5.7	43,710
New Hanover	720.40	67,380	8,950	6.1	86,506
Northampton	38.27	4,590	1,040	7.9	12,331
Onslow	195.56	32,350	2,090	4.1	39,474
Orange	265.94	47,870	3,110	1.9	71,672
Pamlico	34.77	2,550	630	6.5	7,241
Pasquotank	145.43	12,420	1,120	5.3	17,120
Pender	40.50	6,010	840	6.5	18,893
Perquimans	40.85	1,720	210	5.5	6,256
Person	80.17	11,350	4,510	6.0	15,559
Pitt	179.09	53,590	9,580	2.7	60,374
Polk	67.15	3,790	1,030	2.7	10,597
Randolph	144.25	44,540	24,180	2.9	57,369
Richmond	95.28	17,240	6,960	10.3	25,140
Robeson	117.40	41,690	17,430	9.5	56,593
Rockingham	154.74	33,910	15,510	4.8	43,301
Rowan	230.10	41,050	13,150	3.7	65,586
Rutherford	103.91	25,570	12,630	6.0	29,247
Sampson	52.52	14,700	4,980	6.1	28,250
Scotland	109.67	17,130	8,000	7.6	17,572
Stanly	135.00	21,200	9,490	6.2	30,655
Stokes	89.55	6,440	1,730	2.9	23,127
Surry	121.53	35,820	16,500	5.1	35,113
Swain	21.84	5,320	1,120	19.8	8,023
Transylvania	71.84	9,690	3,090	4.2	18,477
Tyrrell	9.49	610	100	11.0	2,161
Union	152.61	34,840	13,220	2.7	51,521
Vance	149.08	18,390	6,210	9.0	18,242
Wake	598.67	280,910	28,190	2.4	280,314
Warren	40.67	3,820	1,210	9.4	10,328
Washington	40.78	3,170	320	11.4	7,553
Watauga	125.61	18,490	1,440	3.6	28,654
Wayne	200.10	39,110	7,520	5.4	43,558
Wilkes	80.94	25,520	9,590	5.0	34,963
Wilson	182.42	34,750	8,190	9.7	35,390
Yadkin	97.94	8,270	3,300	3.1	16,569
Yancey	51.80	4,240	1,840	5.7	12,352

Democrats	Republicans	Active physicians	Hospital beds	Prison admissions; Parole population	Traffic accidents; Fatalities	Live births	Deaths
28,594	14,474	30	107	227; 204	2,443; 33	1,421	810
4,814	658	6	0	11; 13	329; 4	115	111
14,185	5,593	34	127	165; 187	1,376; 8	695	449
21,129	5,620	35	233	278; 181	1,613; 14	877	648
15,835	12,743	22	75	123; 135	1,183; 10	725	487
11,909	6,614	21	65	46; 60	1,117; 10	446	370
—	—	18	83	35; 26	447; 6	250	322
7,084	3,795	7	0	14; 14	322; 4	209	190
10,581	2,084	12	49	96; 87	770; 7	332	271
158,367	125,409	483	1,756	985; 1,642	23,206; 63	8,719	4,102
1,353	7,532	11	40	24; 12	266; 2	162	179
8,752	3,543	9	8	170; 103	526; 7	362	241
15,540	17,772	31	267	170; 171	984; 21	823	751
27,232	13,750	50	241	219; 230	2,397; 29	1,200	828
42,671	33,998	106	524	400; 457	4,957; 11	1,802	1,146
11,619	540	7	0	96; 86	401; 7	278	266
22,175	12,794	62	133	233; 189	3,200; 25	3,157	628
43,547	16,606	389	575	153; 140	2,362; 11	1,143	574
5,211	1,510	5	0	41; 26	198; 7	129	132
11,940	3,547	24	130	116; 101	808; 11	453	353
12,024	5,336	13	43	68; 72	649; 10	437	298
4,784	958	2	0	19; 22	204; 5	113	121
11,839	2,906	11	41	96; 69	850; 6	402	359
38,604	15,776	209	560	335; 1,618	3,743; 24	1,700	943
4,891	4,340	8	26	19; 19	299; 2	160	224
20,738	31,187	32	107	222; 238	2,723; 32	1,547	936
19,914	3,930	19	—	167; 175	1,231; 15	667	540
50,142	4,886	45	226	334; 513	2,623; 43	1,940	1,115
28,130	11,444	46	202	301; 276	2,157; 17	1,194	945
30,710	28,446	61	203	357; 303	2,677; 24	1,509	1,273
18,706	8,562	29	100	129; 178	1,351; 15	820	640
16,437	10,565	23	116	141; 152	1,283; 27	705	568
12,579	2,928	26	106	172; 132	795; 8	572	319
15,027	12,381	25	107	92; 74	1,053; 10	685	551
11,108	10,488	7	53	65; 58	736; 6	518	364
19,143	13,089	36	184	167; 152	1,934; 21	802	698
5,042	2,206	10	24	12; 8	124; 0	182	120
8,969	7,240	18	54	33; 35	407; 5	276	294
1,901	198	2	0	4; 16	137; 1	27	34
25,628	20,234	32	160	219; 970	2,409; 29	1,612	698
15,487	2,114	21	83	168; 243	1,071; 14	617	453
145,627	97,652	408	1,137	1,039; 1,075	16,796; 48	7,653	2,825
9,283	774	10	0	50; 44	284; 9	234	212
6,453	823	4	49	38; 57	339; 3	178	171
11,626	12,186	26	123	45; 36	1,331; 6	358	266
28,683	12,348	52	216	270; 1,484	2,375; 20	1,602	920
12,508	19,875	28	120	160; 146	1,473; 13	770	511
24,520	8,814	30	182	168; 258	2,075; 16	976	751
5,695	10,005	12	46	58; 49	750; 10	423	311
6,544	4,803	9	8	11; 13	231; 0	178	141

Bibliography

Business North Carolina. "1996 Business Handbook: A Comprehensive Look at the Tar Heel Economy—and the Work Force That Is Shaping It." *Business North Carolina, Special Issue* (February 1996).

Corbitt, David Leroy. *The Formation of the North Carolina Counties 1663–1943.* 2nd printing. Norcross, Georgia: The Harrison Company, 1969.

Crouch, John. *Historical Sketches of Wilkes County.* Chapel Hill: University of North Carolina Press, 1983.

Heatherly, Charles. *Courthouses of North Carolina and Tales that Whisper in the Stone.* Norcross, Georgia: The Harrison Company, 1988.

Hubbard, Fred C. *Old Town: When Wilkesboro and I Were Younger.* North Wilkesboro, N.C.: Carter Hubbard Publishing Inc., 1988.

Jackson, Ronald Vern and Gary Ronald Teeples, editors. *North Carolina 1830 Census Index.* Bountiful, Utah: Accelerated Indexing Systems, Inc.; Provo, Utah: Dana Press, 1976.

Lefler, Hugh Talmage and Albert Ray Newsome. *A History of a Southern State*: *North Carolina.* Chapel Hill: University of North Carolina Press, 1953.

Moore, Elizabeth Vann. *Historic Edenton and Chowan County.* Edenton's Woman's Club, 1989.

North Carolina Administrative Office of the Courts. Project of the School of Design, North Carolina State University. Robert P. Burns, Project Director. *100 Courthouses: A Report on North Carolina Judicial Facilities*. Raleigh, 1978.

North Carolina Atlas & Gazeteer. 2nd ed. Freeport, Maine: DeLorme Mapping, 1993.

North Carolina Department of Cultural Resources. Division of Archives and History. *Guide to North Carolina Highway Historical Markers*. 8th ed. 1990.
_____*National Historic Landmarks in North Carolina*, 1996.
_____*National Register of Historic Places*, 1995.

North Carolina Office of Budget and Management. State Data Center. *Profile of North Carolina Counties*. 7th ed., 1986.

North Carolina State Board of Education. Department of Public Instruction. *Education Directory, 1996–1997*.

Puetz, C. J. *North Carolina County Maps*. Puetz Place, Lyndon Station, Wisconsin: County Maps, Thomas Publications, n.d.

U.S. Department of Commerce. Economic Statistics Administration. Bureau of the Census. *North Carolina Census of Population and Housing Unit County, North Carolina 1940–1990*. Washington, D.C., 1990.

Wellman, Manly Wade. *Dead and Gone*. Chapel Hill: University of North Carolina Press, 1954.

West, John Foster. *Lift Up Your Head, Tom Dooley*. Asheboro, N.C.: Down Home Press, 1993.

Index

Alamance Comm. College, 4
Albemarle, 107
Albemarle, Duke of, 107
Alexander, William J., 5
Algonquian Indians, 32
Anson, Lord, 7
Anson Comm. College, 7
Appalachian State Univ., 123
Asbury, Louis H., 80, 104
Ashe, Gov. Samuel, 8, 17, 97
Asheboro, 97
Asheville, 17
Augustus, William, Duke of
    Cumberland, 38
Avery, Col. Waightstill, 9
Baker, David, 81
Bakersville, 81
Baldwin, James J., 31
Barber-Scotia College, 21
Barton College, 127
Barton, Harry, 6, 38
Bayboro, 90
Beaufort, 25
Beaufort County Comm. College, 11
Belmont Abbey College, 51
Bennett College, 57
Bern, 37
Bernard, German, 66
Bertie, James and Henry, 12
Bladen Comm. College, 14
Bladen, Martin, 14
Bolivia, 15
Boone, Daniel, 44, 123, 128
Boone, Kyle, 75
Brevard, 112
Brevard, Col. Ephriam, 112
Brevard College, 112

Brunswick Comm. College, 15
Bryson City, 111
Bryson, Col. Thaddeus Dillard, 111
Buncombe, Col. Edward, 17
Burgaw, 92
Burns, Capt. Otway, 129
Burnsville, 129
Butner, Fred W., Jr., 49
Cabarrus, Stephen, 21
Caldwell Comm. College and
    Technical Institute, 22
Caldwell, Joseph, 22
Camden, 24
Campbell Univ., 60
Cape Fear Comm. College, 85
Carteret Comm. College, 25
Carteret, John, Earl of Granville,
    25, 55
Carthage, 83
Caswell, Richard, 27
Catawba Indians, 28
Central Carolina Comm. College, 72
Central Piedmont Comm. College,
    80
Charlotte, 80
Charlotte Sophia, Queen, Duchess
    of Mecklenberg, 80
Cherokee Indians, 31, 54, 68
Chowan College, 64
Cleveland, Col. Benjamin, 34
Clinton, 105
Clinton, Gov. DeWitt, 105
Coastal Carolina Comm. College, 87
Coble, H. L., 49
College of the Albemarle, 91
Columbia, 113
Columbus, 96

Columbus, Christopher, 36, 96, 113
Compton, James, Earl of
    Northampton, 86
Compton, Spencer, Earl of
    Wilmington, 85
Concord, 21
Cornwallis, Gen., 74
Craven Comm. College, 37
Craven, Lord Proprietor William, 37
Currituck, 40
Danbury, 109
Dare, Virginia, 41
Davidson College, 43, 80
Davidson County Comm. College,
    43
Davidson, William Lee, 43
Davie, William Richardson, 44
Davis, Jefferson, 81
Dobson, 110
Dobson, Col., 110
Duke Univ., 46, 88
Durham, 46
Durham, Bartholomew, 46
Durham Technical Comm. College,
    46
East Carolina Univ., 95
Echols-Sprager & Associates, 27,
    43
Eden, Gov. Charles, 32
Edenton, 32
Edgecombe, Baron Richard, 48
Edgecombe Comm. College, 48
Eduardo Catalano & Peter Sugar, 57
Elizabeth City, 91
Elizabeth City State Univ., 91
Elizabethtown, 14
Elon College, 4

Fayetteville, 39
Fayetteville State Univ., 38
Fleming, James, 31
Forsyth, Col. Benjamin, 49
Forsyth Technical Comm. College, 49
Fowler-Jones Lumber Co., 6
Franklin, 75
Franklin, Benjamin, 50, 75
Gardner-Webb Univ., 34
Gaston College, 51
Gaston, William, 51
Gastonia, 51
Gates, Gen. Horatio, 52
Gatesville, 53
George I, King, 15, 85
George III, King, 80
Goldsboro, 124
Graham, 4
Graham, Gen. Joe, 4
Graham, William A., 54
Greene, Gen. Nathanael, 56–57, 95
Greenville, 95
Greensboro, 57
Greensboro College, 57
Griffin, George A., 21
Guilford College, 57
Halifax, 59
Halifax Comm. College, 59
Hanwood Beche Co., 22
Hardin, Joseph, 123
Harles, Harry J., 50
Harnett, Cornelius, 60
Hartley and Smith, 22
Hay, George Henry, Lord Duplin, 45
Hayden, Wheeler, & Schwend, 67
Hayes, George W., 33
Hayesville, 33
Haywood Comm. College, 61
Haywood, John, 61
Henderson, 117
Henderson, Chief Justice Leonard, 62, 117
Hendersonville, 62
Henningson, Durham, & Richardson, Inc., 115
Henry, Duke of Beaufort, 25
Herman, Thomas B., 56
Hertford, 93

Hertford, Marquis of, 93
High Point Univ., 57
Hillsborough, 88
Hoke, Maj. Gen. Robert F., 65
Hunter, Thomas, 78
Hyde, Gov. Edward, 66
Iredell, James, 67
Jackson, 86
Jackson, President Andrew, 54, 68, 86–87
Jacksonville, 87
James Sprunt Comm. College, 45
Jefferson, 8
Jefferson, President Thomas, 8
John C. Campbell Folk School, 31
Johnson C. Smith Univ., 80
Johnston Comm. College, 70
Johnston, Gov. Gabriel, 70
Jones, Arthur, 91
Jones, Willie, 71
Kenan, James, 45
Kenansville, 45
Kinston, 73
Lafayette, Marquis de, 38
Lane, Joel, 119
Lankford, B. C., 112
Laurinburg, 106
Lee, Gen Robert E., 72
Lees-McRae College, 9
Leitner, Joseph L., 36
Lenoir, 23
Lenoir Comm. College, 73
Lenoir, William, 22, 73
Lennox, Charles, Duke of Richmond, 98
Lexington, 43
Light's General Constr., Inc., 55
Lillington, 60
Lillington, Gen. Alexander, 60
Lincoln, Gen. Benjamin, 74
Lincolnton, 74
Louisburg, 50
Loving, T. A., 48
Lumbee Indians, 99
Lumberton, 99
McDowell, Col. Joseph, 75
McDowell Comm. College, 75
McLaurin family, 106
McMillan, Charles, 72
McMinn, Norfleet & Wicker, 57

Macon, Nathaniel, 75
MacRae, J. A., 65
Madison, President James, 77
Manteo, 41
Marion, 76
Marion, Gen. Francis, 76
Mars Hill College, 77
Marshall, 77
Marshall, Chief Justice John, 37, 77
Martin Comm. College, 78
Martin, Gov. Alexander, 78
Martin, Gov. Josiah, 78
Matthews, W. E., 106
Mayland Comm. College, 81
Meredith College, 119
Methodist College, 38
Milburn, Frank P., 17, 51, 99, 101
Milburn & Heister, 65, 95, 117
Mitchell Comm. College, 67
Mitchell, Rev. Elisha, 81
Mocksville, 44
Monroe, 115
Monroe, President James, 115
Montagu, George, Earl of Halifax, 59
Montgomery, Gen. Richard, 82
Montreat College, 17
Moore, Capt. Alfred, 83
Morgan, Gen. Daniel, 18
Morgantown, 18
Mount Olive College, 108
Munger, Henry, 82
Murphy, 31
Murphy, Archibald De Bow, 31
Nash Comm. College, 84
Nash, Gen. Francis, 84
Nashville, 84
N.C. Agricultural and Technical State Univ., 57
N.C. Center for Applied Textile Technology, 51
N.C. Central Univ., 46
N.C. School of the Arts, 49
N.C. State Univ., 119
N.C. Wesleyan College, 84
New Bern, 37
Newland, 9
Newton, 28
Newton, Isaac, 28
North, Francis, Earl of Guilford, 57

Index

137

Northwest Associates, 22
Onslow, Andrew, 87
Owen, Joseph T., 97
Oxford, 55
Pamlico Sound, 90
Pamlico Comm. College, 90
Peace College, 119
Peagram, J. T., 18
Pender, Gen. William D., 92
Perquimans Indians, 93
Person, Gen. Thomas, 94
Pfeiffer College, 107
Pitt Comm. College, 95
Pitt, William, Earl of Chatham, 29, 95
Pittsboro, 29
Plymouth, 121
Polk, Col. William, 96
Pratt, Charles, Earl of Camden, 24
Queens College, 80
Raeford, 65
Raleigh, 119
Raleigh, Sir Walter, 119
Randolph, Peyton, 97
Randolph Comm. College, 97
Research Triangle Park, 88
Richmond Comm. College, 98
Roanoke-Chowan Comm. College, 64
Robbinsville, 54
Robeson Comm. College, 99
Rockingham, 98
Rockingham Comm. College, 101
Roxboro, 94
Russell, Robert, 21
Rutherford, Griffith, 104
Rutherfordton, 104
St. Andrews Presbyterian College, 106
St. Augustine's College, 119
Salem, 49
Salem College, 49
Sampson, Col. John, 105
Sampson Comm. College, 105
Sandhills Comm. College, 83
Sanford, 72
Scurlock, Miles, 29
Shaw Univ., 119
Shelby, 34
Shelby, Col. Isaac, 34

Simpson, Frank B., 60
Simpson, Herbert W., 25
Smith, B. F., Fireproof Constr. Co., 5
Smith & Carrier, 77
Smith, John, 70
Smith, R. S., 62
Smithfield, 70
Snow Hill, 56
Somerset, Henry, Duke of Beaufort, 11
Southeastern Comm. College, 36
Southport, 15
Southwestern Comm. College, 68
Sparta, 6
Stanly, John, 107
Stanly Comm. College, 107
Statesville, 67
Stephens, Senator John W., 27
Stillwell, Erle G., 76
Stokes, Col. John, 108
Stoneman, Gen. George, 18
Sujjavanich, Surapon, 55
Surry, Lord, 110
Surry Comm. College, 110
Swan Quarter, 66
Swain, Gov. David L., 111
Sylva, 68
Tarboro, 48
Taylor & Crabtree, 48
Taylor, President Zachary, 5
Taylorsville, 5
Thomas, Micajah, 84
Thompson, J. M., 50
Trenton, 71
Tri-County Comm. College, 31
Troy, 82
Tryon, Gov. William, 37
Tyrrell, Sir John, Lord Proprietor, 113
UNC-Asheville, 17
UNC-Chapel Hill, 88
UNC-Charlotte, 80
UNC-Greensboro, 57
UNC-Pembroke, 99
UNC-Wilmington, 85
University Medical and Research Center, 80
Vance, Gov. Zebulon Baird, 17, 117
Vanderbilt, George, 17
Wadesboro, 7

Wake Comm. College, 119
Wake Forest Univ., 49
Wake sisters, 119
Warren, Gen. Joseph, 120
Warren Wilson College, 17
Warrenton, 120
Washington, 11
Washington, President George, 11, 67, 74, 121
Watson, Charles, Marquis of Rockingham, 98
Wayne Comm. College, 124
Wayne, Gen. Anthony, 61, 124
Waynesville, 61
Wentworth, 101
Wentworth, Charles W., Marquis of Rockingham, 101
Western Carolina Univ., 68
Western Piedmont Comm. College, 18
Wheeler, 108
Wheeler & Runge, 8–9, 123, 126
Wheeler, Runge, & Dickey, 97
Wheeler and Stern, 7
White, Gov. John, 36
Whitesville, 36
Wilkes, John, 126
Wilkesboro, 126
Wilkesboro Comm. College, 126
Williams & Associates, 107
Williams, William, 78
Williamston, 78
Williford, A. A., 65
Wilmington, 85
Wilson, 127
Wilson, Louis D., 127
Wilson Technical Comm. College, 127
Windsor, 12
Winston, Col., Joseph, 49
Winston-Salem, 49
Winston-Salem State Univ., 49
Winton, 64
Wolf Associates, 80
Wolfe, Thomas, 17
Wright, Gidion, 110
Wright, Orville and Wilbur, 41
Yadkinville, 128
Yancey, Bartlett, 27
Yanceyville, 27

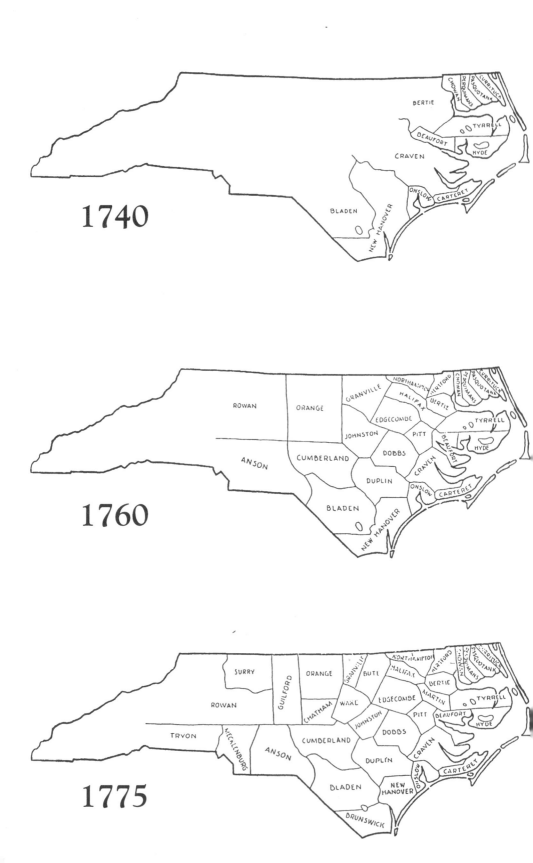